"This exquisitely written book isn't just for those raised fatherless. It's for everyone—male or female, single or married, patchily parenting or poorly parented—who cares to know more about the character of God. Buy it. Give it. Savor it."

REBECCA MCLAUGHLIN, Author, *Confronting Christianity*

"Blair Linne's story reflects our universal longing for a father who will protect and love us. Her aching desire for that earthly father may bring you to tears as her memoir unfolds. Blair's burgeoning faith in her heavenly Father will bring you to worship by the end of this memorable book."

COLLIN HANSEN, Executive Editor, The Gospel Coalition

"This is an extremely timely and beautifully transparent read! Blair invites us in with gospel-ward and hope-filled insight. She fearlessly follows often-severed echoes throughout creation to find the first voice, who spoke all of us into being. She shows us how in real life Christ restores and steadies and answers the deep yearning of every soul by enabling us to know God as our good Father."

KRISTYN GETTY, Hymnwriter; Co-founder, Sing! Conference

"In *Finding My Father* Blair doesn't just tell her moving story; she tells ours. Whether in sorrow, triumph, confusion or breakthrough, the different brushstrokes of our lives paint the same incomplete picture. Every void we'll know can be traced to one veil-tearing truth: we need our Father. This book compels us to not only acknowledge but relish in it; and if we do, nothing can ever really remain the same."

EZEKIEL AZONWU, poet

"The pain of the wound of fatherlessness is hard to put words to, but Blair Linne has done just that. But there is more than just pain in the pages of this book. There is hope and wisdom and an invitation to be loved by a Father who will never disappoint, always provide, always protect, and always be present."

NANCY GUTHRIE, Author, *God Does His Best Work with Empty*

"Blair Linne has a message we need to hear. She has written with refreshing honesty not only about the struggle of growing up in a single-parent Black home but also of the vital role fathers play in every child's life. More than that, Blair has given a message of hope: that there is a Father to the fatherless, and that an intimate connection to him brings the real healing we need. As an inner-city pastor for over thirty years, I have witnessed some of what she writes about, and this is a book I want every family in our church to read—especially the fathers!"

HUGH BALFOUR, Vicar, Christ Church Peckham, London

"On one level, I cannot relate to this book. My dad was the best man at my wedding. On a deeper level, though, I certainly can. Blair Linne and I share the same heavenly Father, so we have far more in common than earthly indicators would suggest. Even the best dads, after all, only dimly reflect the Lord of love. If you are a victim of fatherlessness—whether his absence was physical or relational—this book will be a balm for your soul. Most important, it will crystallize your view of the greatest Father, who turned your criminal trial into an adoption ceremony and has never regretted making you his."

MATT SMETHURST, Managing Editor, The Gospel Coalition

"*Finding My Father* is profoundly substantive and masterfully written. With theological insightfulness and vivid, engaging, and endearing eloquence, Blair puts her finger on the pulse of one of the most critical issues of the day—fatherlessness. By weaving together her powerful personal story with relevant biblical principles and a tinge of strategically placed sociological data, Blair leads hearers to the Father *par excellence*. She presents him as one who not only produces better earthly fathers but also provides a remedy for any who may deal with some sort of 'father wound.' In short, I was riveted. This is a must-read!

WILLIAM "DUCE" BRANCH AKA THE AMBASSADOR,
Musical Artist; Assistant Pastor of Preaching, Southeastern Baptist
Theological Seminary

"This is a powerful book. Pain and a sense of wistful loss surge out of practically every page. A few times I found myself drifting back to my own chaotic childhood, lamenting my own lack of a strong father figure. It's rare to find a book that genuinely moves the soul in the way that this one does. Beautiful. Haunting. Poetic. A book that simultaneously grieves you and heals you. I honestly wish I had the words to convey how much I love *Finding My Father*. What a service Blair has done for the church of Jesus and the millions of fatherless (and motherless) wounded souls that surround us at every level of society. I've already thought of a dozen people I can give it to in my church. And my guess is that you will too."

MEZ MCCONNELL, Author, *Church in Hard Places* and *The Creaking on the Stairs*; Senior Pastor, Niddrie Community Church, Edinburgh, Scotland

"Blair Linne's story about needing, seeking, and finding her father echoes the need we all have to find our true Father and our eternal home. The words on these pages read like a poem, a prayer, a puzzle, and a promise—achingly beautiful, wise, and hope-filled. This book is not only for the fatherless; it's for all of us who are part of the family of God."

KAREN SWALLOW PRIOR, Research Professor of English and Christianity and Culture, Southeastern Baptist Theological Seminary; Author, *On Reading Well*

FINDING MY FATHER

HOW THE GOSPEL HEALS THE PAIN
OF FATHERLESSNESS

BLAIR LINNE

WITH SHAI LINNE

Finding My Father
© Blair Linne, 2021.

Published by:
The Good Book Company

thegoodbook.com | thegoodbook.co.uk
thegoodbook.com.au | thegoodbook.co.nz | thegoodbook.co.in

Cover design by Jennifer Phelps | Art Direction and design by André Parker
Cover photo taken by Marisa Albrecht

ISBN: 9781784986469 | Printed in Turkey

To the fatherless –

*"I will be a father to you, and you shall be sons and daughters
to me, says the Lord Almighty."
(2 Corinthians 6:18)*

Contents

Foreword

John Steinbeck's novel *The Grapes of Wrath* is the story of the disintegration of a family under the withering circumstances of poverty, homelessness, and violence. At the beginning of the novel, Steinbeck presents to the reader the family before they lost their homestead and became unemployed and displaced. He observes that "women and children knew deep in themselves that no misfortune was too great to bear if their men were whole."[1] Steinbeck's simple honesty here is so rare today that it seems to contain insight. In fact, his observation stumbles on a central picture that God has left us about himself in normal human life.

The Bible presents God as our loving Father if we are in Christ. In the Lord's Prayer, Jesus Christ, the second Adam, shows the way back from the tragic sin of the first Adam, who rejected his Creator's wisdom and presence. The Lord's Prayer begins with the recognition of God: he is "our Father." Such an understanding of God is central to the Bible's message, as the second Adam leads us back to the Father we've lost through the ancient sin in the Garden of Eden.

The centrality of fathers and fatherhood pervades the book you are holding. That centrality in Blair Linne's story

---

1 *The Grapes of Wrath* (Penguin, 1992), p 7.

doesn't show itself in the presence of wise and loving fathers, as it did in American sitcoms of the 1950s. Back then, "he's a good family man" was a common expression. Instead, the centrality of fatherhood in Blair's life has shown itself in its widespread absence. "Fatherlessness is the elephant in the room," she writes. "It is rarely talked about but extremely important" (p 34).

In this recounting of a part of her own life story, Blair generously shares with us some of the deepest pains and highest hopes of her own heart. She observes this not with the cool detachment of a research student but with the beating heart of a daughter in search of her dad. As she writes, the truth about the way God made us—with the gifts of gender, marriage, family, childhood, fathers and mothers—shines out. Sometimes it appears in the aches of what Blair didn't have and at other times in the joy of what she found.

The book is written by one who is an artist with words, and we, the readers, get the pleasure of reading it, all ready and prepared for us. In one chapter, the refrain about common experiences in the lives of the fatherless hits the reader: "I did not know it, but I was living it." Blair's prose is as clear as sunshine on a cloudless morning, even when sharing difficult memories. Her writing brings us rich, crisp truths about personal responsibilities, about external difficulties and injustices, and, most especially, about forgiveness and the gospel. This is an absorbing narrative, soaked in biblical wisdom and full of practical help. Blair's own example of humbly receiving God's grace, even through pain, is inspiring, encouraging, and instructive.

Blair's husband, Shai, also contributes to the book, not just by being Blair's husband but by sharing something of his own story, which is both similar to and different from Blair's. And both are very different than the story that they're helping to create for their own three children.

The stories that Blair shares are her own, but they stand for the experience of so many in this fallen world. Whether you know fatherlessness from your own experience or not, this book will inform you and illustrate some of life's most important truths. Blair lets us know her honestly as she puts into words her own disappointment.

In the end, though, her story is one of hope. Through Christ and his church, Blair found her father—and more. I won't ruin the story. It's worth you reading along and letting her guide you through her own experience. As she does—as you read these chapters—I pray that every twist and turn will be used to help you toward the Father you should never miss and who, once found, you can never lose.

I've had the joy of knowing and loving Shai and Blair for years. But by reading this, I've come to appreciate them even more.

Mark Dever
Pastor, Capitol Hill Baptist Church,
Washington, D.C.
June 2021

CHAPTER 1

Partly Cloudy, Mostly Sunny

The section on my birth certificate reserved for my father's name is blank. The inside of the narrow, barren horizontal box has neither been struck through nor erased. It simply lies willfully untouched. So my birth certificate, like many others, tells by omission the story of a mother and father who were never married. This piece of paper was seldom referred to. It almost didn't exist at all, because I almost did not.

Meet Mother. (She is always Mother to me, from when I first learn to speak—never Mom or Mommy.) She is the youngest child of her family. She spends her free time during her high-school years modeling in local fashion shows, brushing shoulders with soul-train hopefuls, and winning the Jabberwock.[2] You'll never find a subject my mother hasn't read up on and doesn't have plans to conquer.

So when Mother finds out she is pregnant with me, she is not ecstatic. She is chained in her second trimester, trying to find a way to pick the lock. She has already known the abrasive reality of being a single mother. Adding to her undisclosed

---

2 The Jabberwock was a scholarship pageant fundraiser for Delta Sigma Theta Sorority.

trials with another fatherless child is not a magazine cut-out she had ever glued on her 80s vision board.

This is why I almost did not exist.

Months before that one-sided information was recorded on my birth certificate, Mother set out to abort me. She had already had my sister at 17, and the thought of raising two daughters on her own at 21 was in tension with her own dreams. But before she went ahead with her plan, she sought out advice from a Baptist minister whose Spirit-filled words convinced her not to go through with it. That's what I'd like to think—or it may have been the fact that by the time she found out, she was too far along in the pregnancy to end my life in our small Michigan town and would've had to travel to a large city like Detroit or Chicago, which made the whole thing too inconvenient. I owe my life to that pastor's words or to those logistical complications.

Apart from a few friends, Mother had little to no support while pregnant with me. She was no longer seeing my dad or my sister's father, and to be pregnant again was frowned upon by our family. My mom's mom—Momma—would have scowled at the news.

Meet Momma. The center of our family, Momma is always busy at service, preparing a plate of food for anyone who stops by. If not ruminating over a cast-iron skillet on how to feed the belly, she is tarrying in prayer for a soul. Her Holy Bible is opened each day by hands which once picked Alabama cotton but now—ever since she headed north in the Great Migration—shovel Michigan snow all winter and then hoe dirt on Good Friday to plant mustard greens and Kentucky Wonders. On Sundays at church, she slides my sister and me a slither of Trident gum, giving us a little something to chew on but never enough to blow a bubble. The fact that my grandmother was divorced and then remarried is confidential information that has been locked away in the memories

(grandma)

of older family members, never to be used in a game of Telephone. Coming up, I know nothing of it. My mother is the result of her second marriage, and my grandfather died when my mother was nine, so I knew nothing of him. Marriage is valued by Momma and so, since my mother has no intention of entering it, there is a problem.

So no, this pregnancy was not celebrated with a yellow Pooh Bear bassinet with a matching Piglet blanket, pink bows, or a smocked dress. During Mother's pregnancy, she was left alone to sit in her own mother's disappointment. And when Mother's body began contracting, she checked into Butterworth Hospital alone. No one was there to hold her hand or tell her it would be ok when she went into labor one brisk November, the day after Thanksgiving.

My mother and father had met at a dance a couple of years before I was born. I like to envision them falling for each other at some point during their rhythmic sways to "Let's Get It On," or being enamored by each other's footwork during the club's mock soul-train line as the DJ changed the vinyl to Michael's "Rock With You." With Grand Rapids being a small town where everyone knows when you come and go, I imagine that the fact that my dad was from a big city like Chicago felt mysteriously appealing to my mom.

Meet my dad, Dee. He is smooth as suede and, being the eldest of six, a natural leader. With his father absent from his home, he has been the one to enforce his mother's will. He's as rugged as the projects he was raised in. He is brown like a Tootsie Roll, and when people get to know him they soon realize he's just as sweet.

By the time Mother gave birth to me she was no longer dating my father. The relationship had been on again, off again, but now it was permanently off. From what I've been told, it seems like they knew how to press each other's nerves. So when Mother decided she would go through with the

generational trauma

birth, she also decided she would give me up for adoption. Not hours after she had had me, she later told me, I looked her straight in her brown, almond-shaped eyes. I wonder if she saw herself in mine. Maybe the idea of what I could be was ricocheting off of her hopelessness, leaving fragments of delight to soak up some of the disappointment she felt. I'm sure that after they pulled me from her cloven belly I cried like every living newborn, but when they laid me next to her, I just stared at her. What was in that exchange, as we gazed into each other's souls, both looking for answers? Maybe my eyes signaled that I would rather she not let me roam too far, or that God works in mysterious ways and sometimes brings much good out of much sorrow. Whatever, Mother always says that that moment melted her heart toward me.

Mother's cousin convinced my Momma to come to the hospital with her, ungluing Momma's cemented plans. Aided by the words of the doctor who told her, "You don't seem like the type of woman who would give your child away," and her cousin's words, Mother decided she was ok with having two daughters. Still, I don't know that there was much of a celebration when they stitched her stomach after the c-section and the epidural wore off. No pink balloons or confetti that day to my knowledge—but I made it. God threw me a birthday party, and for that, I am thankful.

THE FACTS OF LIFE

One day we were whisked off to southern California, the place where it supposedly never rains. I'm not sure if Mother was running away from the small town or toward her dreams of life in a metropolis. I was three; my sister, seven. We had a one-way Greyhound bus ticket that Mother had purchased in hopes of raising two movie stars. We packed all our worldly goods into several large brown Kraft boxes. I slipped into my faded yellow Care Bear pajamas before the start of our three-day journey. There was $300 tucked in Mother's purse. My dad didn't come, of course.

I don't remember much about those early years of not having my dad in the home. I did spend some time around him. I'm sure he changed a few of my diapers. But the only memory I have of my dad living nearby is of Mother taking me to his house to play, and him coming by sometimes, holding a small, brown paper bag filled with Now and Laters, Sugar Daddys, Bazooka, Fun Dip, Bit-o-Honey, Lemonheads, Mars bars, and candy cigarettes. I would be in heaven. Even though my sister and I had different fathers, mine would still come bearing gifts for her, and for my cousin. He was generous with sugar. Candy must have been my dad's love language, and I loved to speak it with him. I think we believed what I had watched that English nanny sing on our Zenith color TV: "A spoonful of sugar helps the medicine go down."

I have one childhood picture with him. Multicolored beads hang on the ends of my 1980s individual braids, which brush just past my shoulders, with bangs similar to Rick James's. I'm a mix of busybody and beauty. I have a visible glob of bright blue Bubblicious on the left side of my mouth as we gaze into the camera. My dad's dark chocolate skin is weatherworn. Hair naturally formed into a small 'fro. His expression is stoic, the look of a man raised in the Ickes on the South Side of Chicago.

Growing up without my dad was mainly sunny but partly cloudy. The older I got, the more aware of the clouds I would become. I would struggle with authority, poverty, and identity as a result of not having my dad in the home. But for now, I'm just a little girl on a Greyhound bus, heading west, caught up in the wind of her mother's dreams.

During the long trek across the US we eat fried chicken that Momma packed for us in foil and paper napkins even as she pleaded with Mother to stay. I chat with just about everyone on the bus. Our last stop is supposed to be Hollywood but someone advises us to get off in Pasadena, telling us about a shelter there where we can stay for a week. The people at the shelter kindly let us stay for two. The place is homey. The rooms have built-to-last wooden bunk beds and a couple of bright, multicolored granny-square crocheted blankets draped on the back of the couch.

After those two weeks, we get a ride to Hollywood and stay in a motel near Sunset Boulevard for two days. We have so much stuff to carry. But we make it there, and put our things down. Now Mother has to figure out what to do next: we can only stay in the motel two nights, since money is already crepe-thin. The morning it's time to check out, Mother asks the motel owner if we can leave everything we own there until she figures out her next move. The owner refuses. We grab what we can carry and leave all of our other things on the side of the motel, behind a dumpster in the alleyway. And we set off walking and praying.

That day she meets a Nigerian security guard, Ayo. She enters a store to buy orange juice and tells him about our situation, asking if he has any leads. He lets us stay in his two-story home off of Arlington Avenue, the color of a pickle. Mother uses his gray hatchback and returns to the motel to get our things, which the motel owner has set aside for us after all.

Ayo has a thick accent and is kind. He treats us to McDonald's Happy Meals and we try fufu for the first time. That Christmas, the tree is surrounded by packages wrapped with snowmen and candy-cane wrapping paper, with our names written on them.

I like it there. But after being there a few months, little do I know, Mother begins planning our exit. Later, she would tell me it was because Ayo tried to hit on her and she wasn't interested in reciprocating, so he told her we had to leave.

Shortly after the ultimatum, Mother is driving Ayo's hatchback and, driving precariously close to the car in front of her, bumps it, leaving a dent. The woman and Mother jump out of their cars. I look on from the backseat. The woman, Aquila, guesses that it'll cost a couple hundred dollars to fix. Mother apologetically asks if there's some other way to make up for the damage. The woman thinks about it for a brief moment and then says, "Well, I do have a stove that you can clean."

So Mother begins working for Aquila, an older Black woman who owns a large home in an upper-middle-class gated community. Shortly after, we move into one of her upstairs bedrooms, which has squeaky unfinished pine floors that feel like sandpaper and scratch the bottom of my feet.

Aquila is kind. She treats us like a grandmother would. At night, she keeps a lump of dark tobacco under her lip, which looks like watery molasses when she lets it fly loose into her spittoon next to her bed. She is tender and always cooking food. Mother cleans her house and takes care of her ailing older sister, which covers our room and board.

But soon we move on again.

We slept under five different roofs that first year and a half before Mother was approved for our own apartment. It's hard to have normalcy with that type of instability. Between our initial expedition to Los Angeles and being old enough to pay for my own apartment, I moved 25 times. We jumped from shelters to strangers to friends' homes like we were playing a game of hopscotch, minus the amusement. I did not know back then that fatherless children are four times more likely to experience poverty than children in a two-parent household. I did not know it, but I was living it.

Mother was all I knew. She was how I interpreted life, the world, safety, and God. When I thought, I tried to envision her thoughts, since "mom is always right." Even when she is wrong, if she says she's right, then she's right, right?

For a kid in a fatherless home, the worst thing someone can say on the playground is "yo momma." I don't ever remember anyone ever saying, "yo daddy." But "yo momma?" Those are fighting words, because she is the one who keeps you alive.

It's Mother who once (or maybe more times than I realize) misses a meal so that my sister and I can eat. She brings two seahorses in a small glass aquarium to my kindergarten class. She watches baby chicks hatch along with me and engages with Ms. Smith at Arlington Heights Elementary School, where she volunteers as the teacher's aid. Mother packs up our laundry and walks us a mile away to the laundromat at dusk. She is the one who prays that the check will clear as our groceries touch the moving belt. Most of the time it does; a few times we leave the store empty-handed. When things work in our favor, we sometimes pack the groceries in the cart and roll it right past the parking lot to our apartment building. When we can't make use of a shopping cart, Mother's palms and my sister's are pinched from doubled plastic bags filled with groceries from Boys Market. We walk those ten long blocks while I complain like the children of Israel in the wilderness, because my single bag containing one loaf of bread is such an inconvenience.

Aged seven, I take up stealing. I try to stuff a long Now and Later pack into my slouch socks and eventually manage to slide it instead into the back pocket of my lime-green culottes. The owner watches me through the mirror placed on the back wall near the candy aisle. The security guard makes all of us go to the backroom and threatens to call our parents. The thought of my mother finding out scares me enough to cure me of the taste of the stealing bug, snatching it out of my mouth. I nervously turn my thin pockets inside out, returning all the candy, and we leave the store with a warning. My sister and her friends berate me because it was my sloppiness that got us caught.

I am good at getting caught. I get suspended in junior high for passing around a poem that threatens the life of my math teacher, Ms. Brown. I didn't create the poem; my friend Hector did. But my background in theater allows me to quickly memorize it, encouraging Hector to print out copies in computer class. We pass it around to whoever is walking through the hallway. Someone gives one to Ms. Brown, who calls the police. We learn within an hour that what was a joke to us turns out to be a serious threat. Hector and I are taken from school to the police station. We sit in an interrogation room, sweating nervously for a few hours with no parental supervision, until they decide to take us back to school.

I did not know back then that the less interaction someone has with their father, the more likely they are to commit crimes and have contact with the juvenile-criminal system. I did not know it, but I was living it.

So it's just me, my sister, and Mother. Mother is what people call a "strong Black woman." She juggles doctor's appointments and dreams; she takes us to revivals at storefront churches around South Central and to parent-teacher conferences. She is constantly questioned by family and friends about coming back home. She feels the shame of pulling out paper food stamps during a season when work is too hard to find. She pays out of already-vacant pockets for charm school, which teaches my sister and me how to walk with a book on our heads and how to tap the seat of the chair like a bumper with the back of our legs before sitting down gingerly, crossing our legs at the ankle and resting our feet to the right side while clasping our hands and laying them on our laps. When she finds herself with a little extra cash, she takes us out of our hood to an upscale restaurant, allowing us to practice our new-found skills while sipping on Shirley Temples. She fights for us to attend the best public performing-arts schools, and she takes me to the craft store to buy large needles and red yarn and then teaches me to knit when I play Madame Defarge in *A Tale of Two Cities*. She researches camera-acting classes, headshots, and how to get an agent, allowing me to get my first one at nine. We go from school to auditions at multiple film studios on the bus. One time, when in order to film a Pizza Hut commercial I have to join the Screen Actors Guild, she uses our rent money to secure my membership. The money allows me to star in that commercial, but the unpaid rent gets us evicted.

My dad was never there to absorb these difficulties that made my mother blush. She carried those burdens alone. She juggled caring for our needs and disciplining us and earthquakes and homework and payment plans to keep the utilities on.

She was all the parenting I had. Because of that, on Father's Day I would often give her a card, thanking her for all of the sacrifices she made for us. I looked at her as a two-in-one. By now, my dad was more a series of blurry snapshots fragmented in the chronicles of my mind than a flow of continuous film.

Truth is, Mother sacrificed so much. But I should've reserved my praise for her for Mother's Day, because all she will ever be is my mother. And that's enough. She gave us all that she had. But she could never replace my dad—nor should she.

For understandable reasons, our culture tells us every day that women like her *can*. This world pushes for a merging of parental roles. The media portrays men as inept, while women are warriors—especially Black women who carry "Black girl magic" in their pockets, allowing them to bear up under any challenge with ease (an apparent compliment often used to dismiss a Black woman's pain and humanity). Some women hint or shout out that they don't need a man or a father. I know from experience that these things are usually said to cover the hurt: *I will say I don't need you before you show you* _don't need me._ But despite all that, the truth is that men are important and dads are needed. Mothers have a different calling than men. My mother was never created to take my dad's place, any more than he could have taken hers.

PERFECT STRANGERS

"Come talk to your dad on the phone," Mother says to a twelve-year-old Blair. My mouth talks, but my fatherless mind roams. He is my father, but he is 2,000 miles away and we only speak a few times a year for a few minutes each call. He's never paid child support. He is never quite committed enough to visit me in Los Angeles. I only see him when we fly or take the three-day train back to Michigan to visit family. He's my father, but he doesn't know that I write poetry, that I like to walk across the street to Bimbos Market and exchange $.50 for a honey bun after school when I can find the quarters, and that I have a sore (that comes and goes to this day) in the corner of my eye from the smoke from watching the National Guard troops drive army tanks down Washington Avenue during the L.A. riots. It's all weird. I think I know what a dad should be, and it isn't the mix of silence and grandiloquent soundbites coming from his end of the call. At twelve I know that this isn't what a dad should be for his daughter, but when I look around, this (or worse) is all I see. When I look around at the men in my South Central neighborhood, it's only cloudy, or stormy. Around the corner from us, I see young men beaming with pride because they belong to Black P. Stone,[3] never because they've been told they are going to be a father.

Below us in our apartment building, Rose drinks Cisco every day like it's water. She doesn't taste the alcohol so much after all these years, but I smell it on her breath. Her man

---

3 A division of the Bloods, a street gang in some parts of Los Angeles.

fights her. Their three adopted boys empty broken glass into the dumpster every month like they work at a recycling plant. Aged twelve, I think to myself, "Why do they keep buying glass furniture? And why does she think this is love?" I still remember the way those boys hung their heads.

My mom and I visit another apartment in the building to play Spades with a married couple. While my mom is in the bathroom, I quietly hover near the kitchen and see Mary on the receiving end of a wet dishrag to the face. When my mother comes back from the bathroom I have tears in my eyes and tell her what happened. They deny it, of course.

This couple from Florida would remain etched in my memory. He made the best conch fritters but also abused his wife. I tucked it away and promised myself that I would never have a marriage like that. I sensed that there must be more to manhood than this. Yet the man who should have been teaching me what manhood is was on the end of the phone. So I rolled my eyes, shrugged my shoulders and said, "Hi, dad."

He would always fill our conversation with a slick saying. He had a way with words, yet we would tread only in shallow waters. He would say, "Stars don't need no polish; they always shine." And I often felt like blurting out, "Why aren't you HERE?" Or, "Maybe I do need polish. I need you. You would know that if you were here." But fear kept my mouth muzzled and my voice muted. I just smiled, afraid that if I told him my honest concerns, then I risked losing the brief interactions we did have. I thought, "At least he says sweet things. He calls me a star. If he stops calling, all I will be left with is silence as he evaporates into the windy city." As I said, growing up without my dad was mainly sunny but partly cloudy. The negative impact of not having a dad in the home is like having to be content with brass rather than gold. And the trouble with brass is that over time the tarnish leaves you green with envy.

LOST

When I was younger, I thought that having my dad in our home would solve all of my problems. I thought that the presence of a father would fix everything that the absence of a father had broken. And I was right to sense that. Studies show that poverty, teen pregnancy, obesity, drug and alcohol use, criminal activity, infant mortality, and behavioral problems are all linked to fatherlessness. And this doesn't even begin to get to the spiritual implications.

But those three boys clearing the glass out could have told me that my theory was not completely true. I know plenty of friends now who did have their dad in the home, and yet it was like he was never there. Truth is, you can *feel* fatherless even while the man who gave you his DNA is living under the same roof as you. Because although he is there, he's not there.

And worse than having a physically absent father is having a present but abusive father. A good friend of mine was molested by her dad from when she was about nine years old. At 13 her dad impregnated her and forced her to have an abortion. From her perspective, it seemed like no one in her family understood—or even wanted to. The man who was supposed to protect and love her instead used her to satisfy his immoral lusts. He then tossed her out like a Raggedy Ann doll to fend for herself. Her dad has always refused to apologize or even admit the ways he sinned against her. I know that many have walked in similar shoes to my friend. They know a life in which their father is more devil-like than dad-like.

We are all, to some extent, the product of our upbringings. And no one grows up in a house free of sin. Whether our dads were there or not, and what they were like when they were there, matters. My dad's absence was the cloud that was always hovering in my sky, sometimes just on the horizon, sometimes blocking the sun, and at other times encompassing me like a fog, blocking me from seeing even an arm's length in front of me. Others had a father whose presence brought storms.

We don't need to hide that father wound. We don't need to pretend that we aren't really *that* affected by our father's absence.

God never tells us to lie about our suffering. He does not expect us to pretend. Christians are not actors. We don't need to be, and we must not be. God doesn't get the glory out of gorgeous lies. When God reads us, it better not be fiction. He only always sees the truth anyway. Not only is he familiar with our families, but he handpicked them (Acts 17:26). So, there are no family secrets with Christ. If anyone should be able to be honest, it should be those of us whose fathers were not what they should have been for us. We of all people are able to say, "Behold, I was brought forth in iniquity, and in sin did my mother conceive me. Behold, you delight in truth in the inward being, and you teach me wisdom in the secret heart" (Psalm 51:5-6). Jesus frees us from any need to pretend.

Hopefully, the reason you picked up this book is because you are willing to travel the hard journey of digging up the layers of unpaved road in order to find a path of healing. God in his wisdom has already mapped out a restorative plan that will remedy the lesions of fatherless sons and daughters. He knows about those pieces of us that are broken, worn, weary and detached from half of our genetic inheritance. He has created a panacea that takes our broken pieces and makes them into something else entirely.

CHAPTER 2

His Name on My Tongue

I was shocked that my son's first word was "dada." Not because I was desperate for him to mutter "mama" first. (Although it would have been a nice treat after the hours of labor, the wrestling with a brimming Diaper Genie disposal system, and the unplanned milk dinner parties at midnight when most people are enjoying their REM. Did I mention the hours of labor?) My shock was because hearing my son connect the word dada to his father caused me to reflect upon my own first interaction with the word.

Back then, the name Dad—or Father, Daddy, Papa, Papi— didn't quite fit in my mouth. Not like Momma's fluffy, buttery yeast rolls that melted in my mouth like cotton candy at every family gathering. Those rolls even had a smell I recognized. Yet "Dad" rested heavy on my tongue like a second language I hadn't mastered. Sure, I could refer to "Dad," but I never tasted what the word meant. "Dad" was a word I sputtered long before I understood it, because he was never at those family gatherings.

As the years began to stack, the sounds of the word hit my ears hollow and moved through me but never went deep enough to mend all of those places in the heart that only a father's care can soothe. Isn't it crazy that you can speak a language and yet certain words do not mean what they should, for lack of experience? The definition of "father" was like describing canary yellow to someone who has never seen a daffodil, a lemon or a New York taxicab. I spoke the language but couldn't fully wrap my tender mind around what a father was in the flesh or in the home.

Fatherhood was something I primarily observed through television shows. Because of that, when I was younger I would daydream. In my mind a father was family-oriented, always coming home from work, lovable, and willing to correct when necessary. My dreams were my attempt to find that missing piece. This dad was a mix of Philip Banks, Andy Taylor, and Cliff Huxtable—never Al Bundy. In real life, though, from my point of view most of the time a father was nothing more than a sperm donor.

When the sun was shining, those clouds went unnoticed. Sometimes it didn't seem to matter. And then it really did.

GROWING PAINS

When I was 13, Mother sat us down and told us she was pregnant. It was by the brother of a neighbor who had become close enough to call family. But this neighbor's brother was someone my sister and I didn't really know at all. We would be three children without our three fathers.

We were excited to welcome a sibling. As Mother's belly began to stretch, she found out that she was having a boy. I was happy for her because I knew that was what she always wanted.

Once those nine months passed, the three of us arrived at the hospital. The triage nurse told Mother that only one guest was allowed. She unapologetically replied, "Well, I have

two children. If they can't be here with me, then I'm leaving!"
They immediately changed that rule.

I went into the operating room with my mother when she
had him. I looked on as they administered the medicine and
pulled up the opaque blue drape separating Mother's top
half from her lower. I saw them slice her open. I saw all the
blood. I saw them pull my 6.6lb baby brother out of her, so
matter-of-factly. The doctor and nurses were smiling. I heard
his newborn cry. Saw them clean away the vernix. I remember
counting to ten, twice. First thing I said to Mother was, "He
has ten fingers and ten toes," because she mentioned that
being a concern a month or so earlier. I was determined to be
the best big sister.

A couple months after I first let his tiny hand grasp onto
my pointer finger, I remember waking up to his cry. This
particular morning looked like many before. I changed and
fed him. I patted his back until he let out a big burp, changed
him again, and laid him back down. I got myself washed up
and ready for school, grabbed my backpack and jetted the six
blocks through our neighborhood, The Jungles, to wait for
the school bus which would arrive at 6:45 a.m.

The summons I received later that day to come to the
school attendance office directly following recess didn't strike
me as strange. But the words I heard on the other end of the
ivory-corded rotary phone would change my life forever.

"Noooooooooo!"

"Nooooooooo..."

It was the only word—the only scream—that my body
could release. My brother was dead. My beautiful baby
brother with curly hair I loved to slick down with Johnson
and Johnson baby oil. He was gone. My brother, to whom
my sister playfully sang TLC's "Baby-Baby-Baby" to stop him
from crying, had no more life in his body.

They called it Sudden Infant Death Syndrome. I did not

know back then that father absence increases the infant mortality rate. I did not know it, but I was living it.

A teacher was in the attendance office as I howled. She offered to drive me to Brotman Hospital. I don't remember what we talked about as we rode together for those ten minutes. I do remember when I saw him lifeless, stiff, and cold. I remember how he smelled at the morgue. There was a metallic smell that I didn't know then but that would haunt me for the next few years around March, the month he died. I didn't know that the sensibility of grief would surprise me while in English Lit., making me feel like I wanted to vomit. Didn't know it would come in like a flood, forcing me to run out of the class overwhelmed with sorrow and ruptured tears. I didn't know then that I would be tormented by his heart which beat no longer.

My mother made arrangements at the funeral home. We drove downtown to pick out a powder-blue suit and white patent leather shoes for a two-month-old. We had an open casket with sky-blue and white flowers, and a shiny blue ribbon that read "Son and brother" in silver shimmer. His dad slipped in and out of the wake like an undercover agent trying not to be identified. I don't think he stayed for the funeral. Later I found out why. He had a family he already belonged to, including a wife. Right before they closed the casket, I broke down in grief like a dam folding under the weight of years of water pressure. I was trying to be extraordinarily strong for a 13-year-old, but grief notified me of my limitations.

He was cremated. His ashes were funneled into a walnut box with the first five letters of the alphabet on five of the six sides, and his name printed on a gold sticker placed on the bottom: "Chace Austin Wingo, January 21, 1995 – March 20, 1995." Death is expensive. The emotional cost drained us. The financial cost took up our rent money that month and then some. So we uprooted again.

After my brother died, I started thinking about God, a lot. I thought about God when, in a moment's flash, I wondered if I should take my own life. I did not know back then that children of single-parent homes are twice as likely to commit suicide. I did not know it, but I was living it.

I questioned why my brother had to die and if it was somehow my fault, since I was the last one to lay him down, and then he suffocated. How does a 13-year-old deal with that?

It wasn't just thoughts about Chace I remember going round and round in my head, spiraling up and dragging me down. I thought about the profession of faith I had made four years earlier when I had walked down the aisle, spoken in tongues, and got baptized in my Sunday dress with lavender and light pink flowers. I thought about the way I was cursing people out at school. I thought about how I had just got elected eighth-grade class clown for bagging on my classmates, who thought I was funny because I tortured the rats in science class by feeding them hot cheetos. I thought about how, while I was popular for cracking jokes, only three of my friends from school had come to the funeral. I thought, "What is this all for?" Everything seemed meaningless, yet dreadfully bulky. The inside of me felt heavy, like my soul outweighed my body.

I was a mess. And I was on my way to becoming a statistic, as it turns out. Because the awkward truth is that fatherhood matters, and my lack of one meant that statistics were pointing in one way, especially now that we were in a crisis. Fatherhood matters in innumerable ways that the stats unveil but don't exhaust. US Census Bureau data from 2020 reveals that one in four children are without a father (biological, step, or adoptive) in their home. Fatherlessness is what lies behind many of our societal ills. Having a family structure without a father predicts significantly higher odds of behavioral problems, poverty, crimes committed, and incarceration. Teens without fathers are twice as likely to engage in early sexual activity and seven times more likely to become pregnant as a teen. Children in fatherless homes are also more likely to abuse drugs and alcohol and more likely to experience abuse themselves. And the children of single-parent homes are twice as likely to commit suicide.

Fatherlessness is the elephant in the room. It is rarely talked about but extremely important. Fathers matter. I was experiencing the burden of something I was too young to name, the lack of something I was too alone to understand. My mother was grieving the loss of her son, so we never talked about what my sister and I had lost too. I needed my father, and he was not there.

FAMILY MATTERS

There was so much I did not know growing up, but one of the things that I did know was that fathers were meant to provide for their children. I learned this when my sister received a child-support check in the mail from her father and I didn't. Several times when needs came up—drill-team uniforms, birthdays, school clothes—if my mother couldn't afford them, I would ask my dad. I was often left with broken promises. I stopped expecting my father to provide, although I knew he should bear the responsibility. That lack of provision translated in my mind to a lack of support and care.

Some look at a father's role as *only* that of bringing home the bacon—just as I guess I did back then. Prior to the last 40 years, this was the prominent view—even social scientists often questioned whether, outside of material provision, a father impacted the development of their children much at all. But although that is part of a father's role, we now recognize that this view is far too narrow in its scope. Fathers are not only providers; they impact the life of their children in more ways than we understand. My father tried to show his care from a distance, but who knows how things would have been different if he had been there. How would it have impacted my stability, identity, or even, just perhaps, the life of my brother if we had had a father in the home?

Consider some of the other ways a father impacts his family in his role. Fathers are protectors, prayer warriors, lovers, spouses, friends, disciplers, playmates, nurturers, encouragers, evangelists, moral guides, teachers, leaders, models and providers. Or they are not these things. Either way, their impact is immeasurable. Fathers often engage in a paternal playfulness which imprints important lessons like security, risk, and trust in their children. Fathers contribute to the mental and emotional health of their children.[4] So when a father is absent—whether physically, emotionally or spiritually—it means that the children and mother suffer, but it also means that the community that they are not part of and the church that they are not serving suffer too.

The Bible gives the spiritual reason behind the statistics that state that fathers matter: "father" is a category created by God. God had fatherhood in mind when he created the first man, Adam. But Adam wasn't the first father—God was. We know that God views fatherhood as important because it is the primary way that he describes himself. Fatherhood is heavenly before it is earthly.

Human fathers are made in the image of God and are to reflect his fatherhood on earth (Genesis 1:26-27; 5:1-3; 9:6). They beget children (Genesis 1:28). They are to be the head of their home (1 Corinthians 11:3). They are given a mandate to provide for (1 Timothy 5:8), protect (Ephesians 5:28),

---

4 K. Adamsons and S.K. Johnson, *An Updated and Expanded Meta-analysis of Nonresident Fathering and Child Well-being* in the Journal of Family Psychology, 27 (2013), p 589-599.

and train their children (Hebrews 12:9), making sure not to provoke them to wrath but to bring them up in the nurture and admonition of the Lord (Ephesians 6:4). They are to instill blessing and identity in their children (Hebrews 11:21). As Pastor John Piper puts it, children…

> "… ought to see in their human father a reflection—albeit imperfect—of the heavenly Father in his strength and tenderness, in his wrath and mercy, in his exaltation and condescension, in his surpassing wisdom and patient guidance. The task of every human father is to be for his children an image of the Father in heaven."[5]

This is a high calling and a hard calling. Any man who lives out this biblical sketch for fathers points to the common grace given to all people. But even more beautiful is the Christian father who points their children to that which cannot be attained merely through natural means. A child in that household has a proximity to special revelation—to a glimpse of God—which sets them on a trajectory of being more likely to have God as their Father (Ephesians 6:4; Proverbs 22:6).

The issue at hand is that many of us did not know a father like this. It started with Adam, who was supposed to model his heavenly Father but instead led the human family into sin. Our fathers have followed right behind Adam's error.

We have fathers who do not serve God.

Fathers who have not provided for us.

Fathers who divorced our mothers.

Fathers who are addicted to drugs.

Fathers who are workaholics.

Fathers who prioritize pastoring the house of God over their own house.

---

5 www.desiringgod.org/messages/fathers-who-give-hope. Accessed May 25, 2021.

Fathers who say they are believers but use Scripture to control others.

Fathers who cheat on and disrespect mothers.

Fathers who do not pass down to us a sense of identity.

Fathers who verbally, physically, or sexually abuse us.

Beyond the sins of our fathers, some fathers have also been sinned against. Some have faced social ills and systemic injustices that have left them discouraged in their manhood and defeated in their parenting. When we ask, "What happened to our fathers to take them off-course from the path God ordained for them?" the answer is, "Sin is what happened," whether that fleshes itself out in systemic injustices or spiritual consequences.

Whatever the specific cause of a home without a father, fatherlessness itself is always, one way or another, a consequence of living in a fallen world. And it leaves us—far, far too many of us—having to provide for, protect, teach, and lead ourselves.

ROOTS

We need to hit pause and consider how it is, and why it is, that close to 70 percent of African American children in the US are born into unwed homes. Notice I said unwed homes—not all of these children are without their father. But because of the high number of Black children in unwed homes, some people make fatherlessness the reason for the Black community's problems. Or, to put it more provocatively, some suggest that there is something about Black people that causes the problem of fatherlessness to be endemic in Black communities. We need to talk about this.

I have had the privilege of visiting the National Museum of African American History and Culture in Washington D.C. three times. One of the exhibits that stood out to me was a journal and ring once owned by Reverend Alexander Glennie of South Carolina. This expandable ring had been used in over 400 weddings of enslaved persons, and their names are documented in his journal. This was during a time when the enslaved were not legally allowed to marry. Yet they chose to exchange vows before God in a Christian ceremony.

There is plenty of evidence that family has always been valued by Black people, despite those families always being liable to be torn apart and sold. In Frederick Douglass's autobiography, *My Bondage and My Freedom*, he speaks of the effects slavery had upon fatherhood and likewise the family:

> "Slavery does away with fathers, as it does away with families. Slavery has no use for either fathers or families, and its laws do not recognize their existence in the social arrangements of the plantation. When they do exist, they are not the outgrowths of slavery, but are antagonistic to that system."[6]

After Emancipation, thousands of freed people who had been unable to legally marry prior to the Civil War validated their union before God through the Freedmen's Bureau and local reverends and governments. There were thousands of ads published in newspapers by African Americans looking to find family members they had been pried from. "In 1865, a reporter for *The Nation* met a man who had walked 600 miles from Georgia to Concord, N.C., in search of his wife and children."[7] Not all who were searching found the ones they were looking for; as determined as they were, the shrapnel of slavery still ripped through the Black family, and many of those people had to simply start all over again in order to establish a new family. But there is no doubt that family mattered.

---

6 *My Bondage and My Freedom* (Yale University Press, 2014), p 38.

7 https://college.unc.edu/2012/05/helpmefindmypeople/. Accessed May 25, 2021.

Despite the fact that they experienced a systematic disruption of their inherited culture and the decimation of their family structures—despite Jim Crow laws, redlining,[8] unequal school funding, voter suppression, and other obstacles—still family was a pillar in the Black community.

Even during World War 2, because of the upholding of those Jim Crow laws, the US army ruled that Black soldiers based in Britain were not allowed to marry white English women, and partly as a result of that some 2,000 multiethnic babies were born out of wedlock. Many were raised by single mothers, and others were put up for adoption—yet many of those children were never then adopted, due to prejudice against adopting outside your own ethnicity.[9]

Not only do systemic issues impact fatherlessness but economic opportunities do as well. When the capacity to provide is seen as the identifying trait of fatherhood, employment will impact whether or not a father remains in the home:

> "The 'provider role' is not just something American men *do*, it is a significant portion of their identity, of who they *are* as men. Men, black or white, have difficulty trying to assume the responsibilities of a husband and father unless they are meeting the societal and instrumental requirements associated with being a 'provider.'"[10]

---

8 "Redlining" was a Democrat government policy which began under the New Deal in 1933 and continued to 1977, providing home loans throughout American cities. They mapped neighborhoods and color-coded them based upon the proportion of Blacks living in those areas. Those areas with high numbers of Black people were mapped in red, and were then denied access to home loans, which created Black ghettos, incentivized segregation, made the fear of Black people financially reasonable, and contributed to the racial wealth gap.

9 Lucy Bland, *Britain's "Brown Babies": The Stories of Children Born to Black GIs and White Women in the Second World War* (Manchester University Press, 2019).

10 Ed. Roberta L. Coles and Charles Green, *The Myth of the Missing Black Father*

In the 1940s and onward, the number of agricultural and service jobs began to contract, leaving many Black men unemployed. Welfare became a help to eliminate hunger by feeding starving bellies as a result of this unemployment—but it also became a huge catalyst for pushing men out of the home. Provisions enforced in urban areas stated that if a man was found in the home, the mother would lose her welfare benefits. The fear of raids caused many poor women to discourage their men from being at home. (These raids were not enforced in white communities.) So welfare was an incentive against two-parent households. If a man's role is to provide for his family, and they already have a provider in the government which has pushed him out, why stick around? Men who were struggling to provide for their family would want to stay away, since doing the opposite would take food out of the mouths of their hungry children.

Then there was the drug epidemic of the 1980s and 1990s with the introduction of heroin and crack cocaine—to which my own father fell prey. Rather than drug addiction being viewed as a health crisis (as the current opioid epidemic is), crack was criminalized in what is known as the "War on Drugs." The Black militant presence in many communities of color (which was partly there to protect against the police) began to be replaced by gangs. Those gangs then became distributors of narcotics in a community with depressed economic opportunities. With the increase of narcotics and crime came an accompanying expansion of the police state. This led to an over-policing of urban areas, which has led to the ballooning of the prison population through mass incarceration—which primarily affects Black men. These challenges are not something that every single Black man has experienced (Black people are

(Columbia University Press, 2010), p 21.

not a monolith), but many men—too many men—have. We know that when those men complete their prison sentence, a criminal record keeps them out of decent work and housing, which contributes to the high recidivism rate. But even for those who have never been to jail but simply struggle to find work, "employment increases the likelihood that a young man will marry the mother of his child by eightfold."[11] All these challenges are faced by men in communities that also contain a cluster of issues like failing education systems and certain cultural components which reinforce these particular dysfunctions.

If we want to talk about the 70 percent of Black fathers who are unwed, we have to talk about—and do something about—some of these issues. In order to understand the state of the Black family, we must grasp the experiences of some Black men. However, not all of the issues are systemic—there is the need for personal responsibility. The temptation is to place the blame on one and not the other. Having the "chips stacked against you" doesn't excuse you from what God is calling you to do and gives you the ability to do.

The truth is that fatherlessness is not only an African American issue but a human issue. Black men have been labeled as the poster child for the deadbeat dad, but although Black men are least likely to cohabit with their child's mother, they also have the highest rates of visitation when it comes to their children:

> "37 percent of Black nonmarital fathers were cohabiting with the child (compared to 66 percent of white fathers and 59 percent of Hispanic fathers), but of those who weren't cohabiting, 44 percent of unmarried Black fathers were visiting the child,

---

11 *The Myth of the Missing Black Father*, p 21.

compared to only 17 percent of white and 26 percent of Hispanic fathers."[12]

High rates of nonmarital childbearing occur in Latin America (55–74%), South Africa (59%) and Sweden (55%). So although this issue plagues the African American community in the United States, it impacts other ethnic groups globally too. Fatherlessness cannot be blamed on or predicted by the color of a man's skin. We must do away with this unidimensional portrayal of Black dads as concomitant with fatherlessness.

BEWITCHED

This is an issue that impacts all of us. This is because the issue is not merely systemic—it is spiritual. One thing I have heard my husband, Shai—who grew up in a similar situation to mine—say is that we are all victims and rebels. Victims because we have all been sinned against by others, whether systemically or through the sins of our fathers passed down to us; and rebels because we have all sinned against God. We have to accept the fact that we live in a fallen world. The idea that our lives should fit in a box wrapped in a neat existential bow was done away with once Adam helped himself to that forbidden crop in Eden. Adam and Eve believed that they could actually cover themselves and their crime with fig leaves. But they could not.

It would be mind-blowing if that fruit that Adam ate was a fig—and that he then used leaves from the same tree to attempt the cover-up. It would be like a two-year-old with a mouth speckled with chocolatey crumbs emphatically shaking his head, adamantly denying the fact that he ate the chocolate-chip cookie. Yes, mankind took the cookie from the cookie jar—but we stand back and say, "Who, me?" We

---

12 *The Myth of the Missing Black Father*, p 8.

ate the fruit, and one of the results is that there has been no perfect human father since—rather, a slew of absent fathers who have followed the man that came long before them but whose original sin affects them. This is a fallen world, and we live in it with sinful hearts. And we face a real enemy who wants to attack our families.

Satan wants nothing more than to kill, steal and destroy all who help spread God's legacy on earth. Proverbs 13:22 says, "A good *man* leaves an inheritance to his children's children" (my emphasis—see Ephesians 6:4, too)—and Satan knows of this call that men have been given, to leave not only a financial inheritance but a spiritual one. So he attacks any man who would be a God-the-Father imitator and aim to leave an imperishable inheritance for his seed. Satan makes every effort to thwart this plan, because he knows if he has the man, he has the woman. If he has the man, he has the children. If he has the man, he has the community. If he has the man, he can wiggle his way into the church. We have believed the lie—his lie—that mothers matter but fathers are dispensable. Satan knows that if he can execute the man, several more caskets will soon trail behind his, "dead in … trespasses and sin" (Ephesians 2:1). The devil's best line of attack against the family is often to get at the father. It is always children who are left reeling and dealing with the consequences of that.

Fathers matter. Of course, having fathers in homes is not the abracadabra which hides the rabbit of sin under the hat. With every magic trick the rabbit must reappear in the end. The rabbit of sin exists. No sleight of hand will get rid of this problem. No government policy or program.

Of course, I want policy to change. It would be a blessing if there were some way to encourage and incentivize men towards marriage, homeownership, and job security. It would help if, rather than private prisons placing a priority on making money, we had more programs aiming to help restore these men who have gone to jail for nonviolent offenses, in order to lower the recidivism rate.

If I had the ability to impact policy, I would advocate for these things. However, I realize that these will only partially remedy the issue. I did not know that back when I just wanted my dad to be *here*. But now I know that I needed far more than his presence. I needed a man who followed God and called me to do likewise.

Policies and programs can help, and should help, but they cannot solve the problem. Only the Father of mercy is sufficient to deal with fatherlessness from its root. He is able not only to get dads back to their families in the home but to bring fathers to himself. This does not happen through magic but through the Messiah. So this is deeper than just saying, "Men, get back to your women and kids." It is about saying, "Men, turn back to the triune God, trust in Christ, and return to the church, because you cannot father in a God-honoring manner without being united to Christ and his bride. You cannot be the father you were created to be without knowing your heavenly Father."

And so it is also saying to teenaged Blair that she did not know what she needed. She needed a dad, yes; but she needed a dad who knew God, and she needed a God whom she knew as Father. Teenaged Blair, it turns out, was wishing for far too little.

LAMENT, REPENT, AND HOPE

In the gospel, we have a Savior who broke the power and penalty of Satan's devices, and will one day break the chain of sin's presence. Until that day, systemic problems are intractable, but spiritual ones are not—because mercy triumphs over judgment (James 2:13).

How does this speak to those of us who grew up without a father? It tells us that we cannot change what happened to our fathers, nor are we responsible for what our fathers have done to us. That is not our responsibility, but theirs. But it also tells us that we are responsible for how we deal with our pain—since that is not their responsibility, but ours.

We have a Deliverer who crushed the serpent's head, and who is able to help us respond rightly to even the most grisly circumstances.

In the book of Lamentations we find people who are broken by the systemic and sinful consequences of previous generations and their own. What do they do? They lament, and they repent. They look back, but they also push forward. They remember that God's mercies are new every morning. They know that a new day is upon them in which there is forgiveness and restoration, and in which they can walk forward in line with God's purposes, even as they groan under the consequences of what went before them.

This is the tension of living in a fallen world. We admit our pain, trauma, and disappointment, and yet they don't have to control us. We can cast our cares on the Lord, knowing that "we do not have a high priest who is unable to sympathize with our weaknesses, but one who in every respect has been tempted as we are, yet without sin. Let us then with confidence draw near to the throne of grace, that we may receive mercy and find grace to help in time of need" (Hebrews 4:15-16).

On the cross, Jesus felt forsaken by his Father. Because of that, he can sympathize with us. And because of that, he can forgive us and through his Spirit transform us.

Whatever our experience of family, we are all victims and we are all rebels. So we lament. We repent. And then, because of God's grace, we look forward with hope.

I still remember a prayer I prayed that year that my brother died. That year that I wanted to die was the same year that I prayed, "God, please bless me with a godly family."

Of course, I didn't understand what I was praying. I'd never known or really even seen that kind of family. I didn't know that "father" is a category created by God. I had no idea that the Bible had much to say about it. But clearly I knew one thing: I was lacking something. What I had to figure out was what that something was.

CHAPTER 3

Fathered from Above

I was 18 when I realized my backbone was no longer made for bending. Prior to that, fear had won for so many years. Now I finally pried off the muzzle from over my mouth and confronted my father's scarceness during one of our sporadic phone calls.

But let's back up to what led up to that call.

Within a two-week period at my "name it and claim it" church, three different guys had all said that God had told them they were to marry me. They weren't at the point of getting down on one knee, but they were very clear about what they thought God was telling them. I wasn't dating any of these guys, and never would, and yet I remember racking my brain over this dilemma. The thought that God would tell these three friends the same thing and not mention any of it to me was strange. Yet I was a Creflo Dollar partner at the time, consumed with the mystical idea of man's ability to speak things into existence—so I took their words to heart.

And that made me consider, for the first time, what I should or shouldn't look for in a husband. I had no idea. I was nowhere near ready to tie the knot.

God used those three guys to stir up in me the realization that not only did I not know what I wanted in a guy, but at the core I didn't know who I was. In order to know who I should marry, I had to understand who God made me to be. This caused me to face another downside to growing up without a father: especially when it came to what to look for in a man, I had no one to model it to me or guide me through these things.

Growing up without a father is like this. We see the *effects* of not having our dad—the gash, the tears, the steady dribble of heartache inside of us; the slow, creeping onset of pain and grief as the breach of relationship begins to boil over into different areas of our life. But what most of us never do is to work our way back to find the original cause. Quickly bandaging the cut and moving on seems easiest. So we put on our "I'm ok" face and keep Pandora's box sealed for fear of what may escape.

But now I was 18, and for whatever reason those three guys' words meant I knew I couldn't keep the box closed. As painful as what was potentially on the inside was, I had to pop the seal. So, on the phone with my dad, I did what I had wanted to do ten years earlier but hadn't had the guts to.

I blurted it out before I could talk myself out of confronting the truth, again. I told him. Told him that I was hurting. That I had been affected by his absence. That I expected more from him than silence. He listened, and said words to me that I never expected. That he was afraid too. That his dad had not been in his life, and now he had repeated the cycle.

I had not created a play-by-play for the conversation in my mind, but this was not panning out like I had thought. And it helped me see something about my dad I had never really considered before: that he was a man. He was just as broken and needy as I was.

I think I had a picture in my mind in which my dad could and should be like a superhero: that he would swoop in eventually to save the day with all the right words. That he wore an S on his chest. Maybe it was all the TV I was watching, my own unrealistic expectations carefully nurtured over the years, or the slick sayings I was used to hearing slide off his tongue like Jello. But he wore no cape. He spoke no parables or metaphors. He couldn't raise memories of what had not been and breathe life into them with his being there. He had no access to a time machine which would allow him to travel back in time to catch dreams before they shattered in a cacophony of fatherless pain on my stone floor. He couldn't reshape what had already been molded like cast iron. He was simply a beautiful, flawed man. He let me see his frailty that day, and it's something that has cuddled my story like a weighted blanket.

A father is a covering. He is a shield from danger. So where do you go when your dad needs a place to hide too?

Some have suggested that we simply do away with the idea of this kind of father, since it has been so muddied by sin. But our sin does not negate the truth God has established. And no sinner can dictate or destroy what God intends. We just need to lift our eyes a bit higher.

I appreciate what the theologian Bruce Ware says about this. He is speaking specifically about abusive fathers, but we can replace "abusive" with "absent" and it is just as meaningful.

"Some who have been affected by abuse can learn
afresh from our Heavenly Father just what true
fatherhood is. I have sometimes heard that those
who grew up with abusive fathers simply need to
remove from their minds the notion of God as Father.
This name for God is a barrier to their relationship
with him, some have said. But surely this is the

wrong solution for a very real problem. Rather than removing 'father' from our Christian vocabulary, and in particular from our naming of God, should we not work at having our minds and hearts refashioned so that our very conception of 'father' is remade by knowing the true Father over all? That is instead of encouraging a distancing from God as Father, with love and sensitivity we should say to those who cringe at memories of their fathers, 'I've got wonderful news for you. <u>There is a true father who is drastically different in so many, many ways, from the father you had. Meet, will you, the true God and Father of our Lord Jesus Christ. Learn from him just what "father" really means, and enter into the fullness of his fatherly love, care, wisdom, provision, protection, and security.'</u>"[13]

There is a true Father who is drastically different in so many, many ways. And he was not the man on the other end of the phone with 18-year-old Blair.

A DIFFERENT WORLD

When I was 22, I found grace—or rather, grace found me. Despite all of my years attending church, singing in the choir, teaching Sunday school, and reciting Scripture-inspired poetry, until then I did not know Christ the person. When the gospel came to me, I initially wanted to reject it. I thought I was already saved, sanctified, and filled with the Holy Spirit. I had defied many of those statistics about fatherless children, and I had taken comfort in the fact that I was different. I was moral: I intentionally said no to drugs, promiscuity, drinking, and gangs. After my brother died, I had stopped cursing and

---

13 *Father, Son, and Holy Spirit* (Crossway, 2005), p 62.

fighting and had started reading my Bible. If my mother bought a beer at the store, I refused to even hold the bag. From my perspective, I was avoiding immorality and wrongdoing. So it was hard for me to accept what the Scriptures said—that I, too, was by nature "dead in [my] trespasses and sins" (Ephesians 2:1). I didn't think I was that bad. I had a whole list of things I didn't do that I thought separated me from my peers. I didn't think the sins I committed were bad enough to deserve eternal punishment in hell. So when I heard the message to take up my cross, deny myself, and follow Jesus, it was received with an eye-roll.

But still the Bible showed me that from nine years old (when I had made a profession of faith) until 22, I had lived in my own strength. I had gotten the most important thing—my spirituality—wrong. I was more focused upon the God who would bless me with things than the God who wanted to bless me with himself. I started to see that God was right. He doesn't lie. When the righteousness of Christ met my self-righteousness, the Spirit swooped in and he quickly demolished my own efforts, showing me that my foundation was built upon myself rather than on him. The Spirit led me to cry out to God for mercy. For the first time, I knew I was a sinner, not initially because I felt like I was or because the world told me I was, but because God is holy and, as I read the letters to the Roman and Ephesian churches, *they* said I was. As I prayed for forgiveness, I was comforted by grace. God showed me that all of the sins I was guilty of deserved punishment, but that through Christ, there was a pardon.

As I began to walk out this newfound relationship with God, I went from seeing God as a genie to a pardoning Judge. So now, when I sinned, I was waiting for him to throw the book at me, as a judge would. I believed that he tolerated me, but that he would reject me the moment I blew it. I was trying to walk out the Christian life without stepping on any cracks. I thought I was accepted by God because of grace, but that I must be kept by God through my own perfectionist ardor. That is not the gospel. I needed God to teach me more of himself: that he is more than a Judge. He is also a doting, grace-filled Father.

In his love, God had chosen to adopt me into his family as his daughter, through faith in his Son, Jesus (Ephesians 1:4-5). I was his child. Problem was, I didn't really understand the full implications of what that meant.

FAMILY TIES

When a child is adopted, their legal status changes, but their own sense of themselves takes time to catch up. They must learn to trust that this family loves them, cares for them, and is committed to them for the long haul. I have heard of children who, after being adopted by a loving family, sneak food into their room for fear that they will be famished like when they lived with their biological family; and of children who keep their bags packed because they are waiting for their new family to abandon them the moment they make a mistake. They have clearly been damaged by their previous experience.

Similarly, many of us have been impaired in our view of our heavenly Father by our experience with our earthly fathers. We have been made free in and through Christ, having been declared children of God, but sometimes we live like we are still under Adam—still in our old home, under Satan our former master, facing death. What would we look like if we believed God's promises towards us and allowed his truth (not our broken experiences or trauma) to ground us in our assurance as his adopted children?

In Ephesians 3, Paul says, "For this reason I bow my knees before the Father, from whom every family [or 'from whom

I am free not enslaved.

all fatherhood'] in heaven and on earth is named" (Ephesians 3:14-15). Paul is approaching God as his Father, and as the Father of all of us who belong to him. He is not speaking of a universal sonship for all people—rather, this is a divine fatherly love for Christians. This sonship is a fulfillment of the promise given to Abraham: "if you are Christ's, then you are Abraham's offspring, heirs according to promise" (Galatians 3:29). Therefore the essence of fatherhood and family is a derivative of God the Father, not the other way around. <u>We tend to look at our earthly father (whether good or bad) and project their example of fatherhood onto God.</u> But it should be the other way around. I needed—we all need—to take time to unlearn some things in order to look at God and allow him to define fatherhood.

Our Father's Love Is Inexhaustible

Our Father doesn't merely tolerate us. He loves us. He is not like the child who buys the toy truck only to abandon it in the bottom of the toy bin a week later. God is not playing a game of cat and mouse with us. He is not fickle. God's fatherly love is inexhaustible.

In his prayer in Ephesians 3, Paul asks…

> "… that according to the riches of his glory [the Father] may grant you to be strengthened with power through his Spirit in your inner being, so that Christ may dwell in your hearts through faith—that you, being rooted and grounded in love, may have strength to comprehend with all the saints what is the breadth and length and height and depth, and to know the love of Christ that surpasses knowledge, that you may be filled with all the fullness of God."
>
> (Ephesians 3:16-19)

His agricultural language here—rooted, grounded—reminds me of Psalm 1. The Christian is a tree with deep roots (our comprehension) planted in rich soil (God's love). It makes me think of a baobab tree, one of the longest-living trees in the world. Its bark is fire-resistant. It produces a fruit that is highly nutritious, and it basically laughs at the dry deserts of Africa and Asia in which it resides. It can reach 60 feet tall and grow 30 feet in diameter. It is anchored in the soil by roots that go some 6 feet deep.

Now imagine that tree is a metaphor for those who've been adopted as God's child. Consider, as I mentioned earlier, that the soil surrounding the tree is God's love. The more we mature in understanding the love of God, the deeper we entwine ourselves in his love and expand our view of it. Roots are strong and persistent. We need to think of the largest acreage of soil we can imagine and realize that God's love is wider, goes deeper. It is longer and higher than our finite imagination can grasp. We need to park ourselves in his soil until our roots grow down farther than we can conceptualize, deeper than we can exhaust. Tap into his living water. Let the roots twist and shimmy into the source of our life, which is God's love. God *is* love. And he loves his children inexhaustibly.

If we believe in Christ, we are one with him and receive the same love, benefits, and fellowship that the Son has from the Father. We now have a loving forever-parent who guides our home, decisions, and life. We can approach him without fear of being rejected, abandoned or ever condemned. Because his perfect love casts out our fear, we can unpack our bags and make ourselves at home with him.

Our Father's Presence is Permanent

"For my father and my mother have forsaken me, but the LORD will take me in" (Psalm 27:10). Parental reluctance or temporal transience is contrasted with, not analogous to, God's faithfulness. Though my father or mother forsake me or are separated from me by death, the Lord will take me in; literally, he will gather me up. He collects waifs in his arms. The presence of our Father is stronger and more certain than that of our natural parent. He will never forsake us or let us down. He will never leave us. Everything about this world changes like the seasons. Even in a particular season, there is change still. So, last week, it was summer here in Philadelphia; one day we had blazing temperatures with high humidity, and the next day we had pouring rain, with quarter-sized hail and strong winds. Sunshine was one change, the rain another, and the unforeseen hailstorm was another change within the changing change. Not so with our immutable God. He gathers us up in his arms of protection, and the tie that he uses to link his heart with ours will always remain. Nothing can break it. God tells us that he is not going anywhere. His is the love that will not let us go.

Our Father Delights in Giving Perfect Gifts

"For everyone who asks receives, and the one who seeks finds, and to the one who knocks it will be opened. Or which one of you, if his son asks him for bread, will give him a stone? Or if he asks for a fish, will give him a serpent? If you then, who are evil, know how to give good gifts to your children, how much more will your Father who is in heaven give good things to those who ask him!" (Matthew 7:8-11)

A harsh taskmaster would not tell us to ask for what we need. The God of deism—powerful but distant—would never say "Seek" because he is far too impersonal. A cruel and profligate dictator would never say, "Knock on my door so that I may bless you." He would tell us to quiet our mouths, keep our heads down, and get back to work. But our God tells us to look up and depend upon him by asking, seeking, and knocking for what we need. Even flawed, "evil" fathers give good gifts. What does a flawless benevolent Father give? *Perfect* gifts. He gives us exactly what we need at every moment. Supremely, he gives us himself, and when we know him as our Father, we discover that we can be satisfied in God.

The challenge of being a child is that our perspective is limited. We often don't know what is the good and perfect gift that we need at a particular moment. But our heavenly Father's gifts are always and only good, even when we did not choose them and cannot see *how* they are good. For those of us who struggle with fatherlessness, we can trust God and know that he withheld our fathers so that we would come to know, love, and appreciate God himself in ways we otherwise would not have. That is certainly my story.

But there's more. God not only delights in giving us perfect gifts; he delights in us:

> "The LORD your God is in your midst, a mighty one
> who will save; he will rejoice over you with gladness;
> he will quiet you by his love; he will exult over you
> with loud singing." (Zephaniah 3:17)

God's joy is uncreated and eternal. It is always directed to his Son. When we place our faith in him and are joined to Christ, we place ourselves at the receiving end of God's constant outflow of delight. "There will be more joy in heaven over one sinner who repents than over ninety-nine righteous persons who need no repentance" (Luke 15:7). From the moment a sinner becomes God's child, he or she enters God's gladness. His gladness is that which burns just as brightly today upon his Son and all who are in the Son as it has in eternity past. It is his joy to save and sustain us. He takes pleasure in loving us.

If you are in Christ, God sings over you. You may have never received encouraging words from your earthly father or heard those three words, "I love you," glide off of his mouth in your direction—but God serenades us, celebrating the fact that we are his. Can you imagine his holy voice, with perfect pitch, tone, and intensity, filling our ears and heart with his joy? His is a greater delight than most fathers have when they first lay eyes on their newborn child. He loves us. He is not bringing up our past sins, for he has removed them as far as the east is from the west. We are his holy children. At the moment of salvation the singing begins, and it will crescendo into a climax when we are with him in heaven.

Our Father Brings Us Up

"The Lord disciplines the one he loves, and chastises every son whom he receives" (Hebrews 12:6). Part of a father's responsibility is to discipline his children. All discipline seems painful, and none of it is pleasant—but, when done rightly, lovingly, and wisely, it is for the child's good. When we are tempted to not listen to God or to stray, he mercifully grabs our attention so that we will not leap out of his arms. Pain and suffering are a means of grace to keep us tethered to God. A rebuke from God—whether through his word, his children or the circumstances he permits in our lives—is a great blessing. It shows that God is not indifferent to us. He is not content with us looking more like our natural selves than our spiritual selves. So he uses our sin, suffering, and pain as a warning to draw our attention to his fatherly care and to make us more like his perfect Son.

Taking the time to consider these and other Scriptures which show me who my Father is and how he sees me changes everything. Now the word "Father" marinades on my tongue. Finding my heavenly Father gives me a renewed understanding of what true fatherhood is. The only way that we can have hope is by shifting our eyes away from what we do not have in an ephemeral father to what we do have in an eternal Father:

> "Blessed be the *God and Father* of our Lord Jesus Christ, who has blessed us in Christ with every spiritual blessing in the heavenly places, even as he chose us in him *before the foundation of the world*, that we should be holy and blameless before him. In love he *predestined us for adoption* to himself as sons through Jesus Christ, according to the purpose of his will, to the praise of his glorious grace, with which he has blessed us in the Beloved."
>
> (Ephesians 1:3-6, my emphasis)

Adoption is what keeps the Christian's heart pumping:

> "Justification [the truth that God now declares us as perfect as his Son, because his Son has taken our sin and given us his righteousness] is the primary blessing, because it meets our primary spiritual need ... But this is not to say that justification is the highest blessing of the gospel. Adoption is higher, because of the richer relationship with God that it involves."[14]

When we come to grips with the fact that adoption is what God was aiming at all along, we realize that the gospel is not only the declaration that a sinner will receive a pardon in a courtroom, but that an illegitimate child will receive a place in the family. We have a place in our Father's house. A permanent place. And it is glorious.

---

14 J.I. Packer, *Knowing God* (IVP, 1973), p 206-207.

GOOD TIMES

That conversation with my dad about his absence when I was 18 seemed to bring us a bit closer together. He had gotten married the year before, and that ironed out some of the wrinkles of his life and brought with it more starch in our relationship. He started calling more regularly—around every two weeks. Things were not perfect—our relationship still existed on a surface level most of the time—but it was something. But more than being appreciative of the new-found connection, I realized that my dad could not be all I needed or make up for all I lacked. Looking back, this was the moment the Spirit started to show me that he was only to be a pointer to the greater Dad. Our conversation was something, but not everything. Neither could he be.

Nor do I need him to be. By faith, because of the life and work of our brother, the Lord Jesus, the Christian has access to the perfect Father. When we pray, we can call out to our heavenly Father. Dad. Papa. Lover of our soul. Our life. Our peace. Our grace. Our deliverance. Abba! I let his name sit on my tongue for a while. I savor it. He is a father to the fatherless. I can ask him for what I need. No human father, whether present or absent, loving or the opposite, is perfect. He will disappoint in one way or another. But I have a perfect Father who will never let me down.

Do you trust Christ? Then your adoption gives you a new Father. Unpack your bags and make yourself at home.

CHAPTER 4

It Takes a Christian Village

"To pull the metal splinter from my palm
my father recited a story in a low voice.
I watched his lovely face and not the blade.
Before the story ended, he'd removed
the iron sliver I thought I'd die from."

(Li-Young Lee)

I married Shai four months after he got down on one knee. Among the invitations that went out, I invited my father to walk me down the aisle. Despite being a Jehovah's Witness who does not often step foot in a Christian church, he gladly came. He was the beaming father by my side, handing off his 27-year-old daughter to Shai on one of the most important days of my life.

I love watching a father walking his daughter down the aisle because of all it represents: a father who has walked along his daughter in life, protecting and shepherding her until he places his precious child into the hands of a man who will take equally good care of her. That wasn't our story, of course. He was there to give me away but had not been there to raise me. But I was hoping that grace and forgiveness could make up for those many years in which I had been left to walk down the aisle of my life alone.

I went from Wingo to Linne and I was now, for the first time, part of a married household. Shai and I knew we wanted children, if the Lord would provide, and more than anything we wanted to raise them in a loving, God-filled home. But coming up, neither of us had seen these things lived out in front of us. In the world we grew up in, the type of picture we had carefully painted in our minds was, to our peers, a social oddity.

One of the problems with growing up in a "broken home" is that you never get to experience a two-parent one. Unsurprisingly, when children from single-parent homes grow up and have their own children, many of them will pass on the cycle of marital instability or not get married at all. Especially when those children come from educationally disadvantaged homes, they are less likely to marry. We tend to copy what we've seen—or (since the soft, secure everyday mundane reality of marriage is unknown) idealize what we've never had. The truth is that marriage and family are God-given and blessings to be pursued and enjoyed—but also that in this fallen world they're not perfect, and they will require living out the gospel, which brings with it realism, repentance, and forgiveness. Sometimes our ideals of marriage must be sacrificed in order to settle into the real covenant of loving your closest neighbor—your spouse. Marriage is hard at times. Some days are good and others challenging. And it's harder if you've never seen it lived out in front of you, with its ups and downs, for better and worse, and richer and poorer, and in sickness and in health, until death.

I needed to shed my theoretical ideals, and I needed to see marriage and family in practice. I needed to see fathering with a microscope rather than a telescope. By God's grace, in the months before I walked down the aisle to marry Shai, I had the privilege of observing a father or two. Looking back, this was God preparing me for my marriage.

DIFFERENT STROKES

During those two months before getting married, I moved from Los Angeles to D.C. While waiting for our basement apartment, which was 16 blocks from the Capitol, to be move-in ready, I lived with one of my soon-to-be pastors and his family for two weeks. It was the first time I witnessed firsthand how a Christian family could and should interact with each other. I watched as this Texan raised-on-a-cattle-farm, cowboy-boots-wearing brother led his wife and kids. I watched as he cared for and provided for them. When it was time for the children to go to bed, I was invited to participate in their nighttime routine. It was sweet, for the first time in my life, to not only observe but participate in family worship led by a man at home. Of course I had observed Momma worship God. She was the first Christian I ever met who would be up before sunrise each day praying fervently and reading her Bible. But I had never witnessed a husband and father lead his family spiritually. These children did not have a perfect father in this man, but they did have one that sought to be present and influential in teaching his children to value Jesus, his word, his church, and their family.

As I settled in, I then began to nanny for another pastor and his family, and I soon realized that what I'd initially observed in my host family was common in many of the other families I was now brushing shoulders with. What was so new to me was simply ordinary for them. I watched this father get up to play with his sons before he left to go work at the church office to serve other families. When one of his sons was having a hard day, I would give his father a call, and he would speak to that son and let him know that he would come home to address him if necessary. He prioritized his family. As I got to know the rest of the church, I observed dads spending one-on-one time with their daughters, encouraging their sense of worth and pouring on their love. I heard of fathers being intentional with their sons by getting up early to read them Bible stories before work. It was a beautiful sight to behold. My church was teaching me what fathering looked like. My church was showing me what we should pursue in our own marriage and, God willing, some ways we could love our children if the Lord were to provide them.

Everyone naturally desires family. Family is necessary for our human welfare. Without male and female coming together to procreate, the entire human race will end. And yet parental responsibility doesn't end there. An infant requires years of nurturing and provision. If a child does not have some form of family, their very existence is in jeopardy. This is true naturally and spiritually.

This is the great gift the local church can offer to those who grew up in homes where Jesus was not Lord, and especially homes where dad was not around—an opportunity to see gospel-shaped marriage and parenting up close. This is a way that a local church can help break the cycle. This is one of the great privileges and responsibilities of being the local church. Many of us who are fatherless have been so used to figuring out life on our own, living in isolation—but in the church God says, *Here is a family to walk with you and help you along.*

ALL IN THE FAMILY

Throughout the Bible, God commands his people to care for the fatherless:

> "Religion that is pure and undefiled before God the
> Father is this: to visit orphans and widows in their

affliction, and to keep oneself unstained from the world." (James 1:27)

God knows that orphans are dealing with affliction. God knows that the fatherless have special needs. I always find it encouraging when God foresees what I will need and places it in Scripture. This is another way that God's omniscience and care for us is put on display. As daughters and sons of God, we are able to find a loving, committed family through the church. Through our brothers and sisters in Christ, we can experience restoration so that we do not repeat the sins of our earthly fathers, nor do we have to be crippled by them.

Genuine "religion" will lead us to a holy life which isn't only about understanding right doctrine or going to a "solid" church but also works itself out practically, with us taking care of those who have been rejected or considered castaways.

The call for the church is clear. God wants to use the church to satiate the fatherless child's deepest longing for family and love. This is why the Scripture says that we should love one another with brotherly affection, contribute to the needs of the saints, and show hospitality (Romans 12:10,13). Our Father is calling us to be family. As we open up our lives and homes to welcome those who come from broken homes, we have an opportunity to show the same love and comfort that God has lavished upon us. Those who have had fathers who faithfully lived out the Scriptures can then model that for spiritual sons and daughters who did not.

It is not enough to purport to love God without exhibiting a tangible love for the church. Growing in maturity is not primarily measured by the amount of information we can retain about God; rather, it is measured by the amount of love we display towards our neighbors, especially the household of faith (Galatians 6:10). Peter wrote in his first letter that we are purified through our obedience, and he outlined what that purity would lead to and look like:

> "Having purified your souls by your obedience to the truth *for* a sincere brotherly love, love one another earnestly from a pure heart."
>
> (1 Peter 1:22, my emphasis)

An emphasis on the family is often missing when we think about our spiritual adoption. God requires us to love both God and people. If one of those two elements are missing, then we are not really doing the other. Christ is the head of his body, the church (Colossians 1:18). God has ordained it so that the head and body work in unison. We need to be careful not to neglect the truth that in redemption not only do we gain God as Father, but we gain the church as our family. The church is meant to be an extended family structure, consisting of spiritual siblings and spiritual parents (1 Timothy 5:1-2). It is not an accident that the Bible uses the word "household" to describe the church (Ephesians 2:19; Galatians 6:10).

In church, fellow believers become our spiritual brothers, sisters, mothers, and fathers. Although we may not have had a dad, we can pray that God will send us a family in our church that will be willing to care for us and provide us with a father-figure who will be the masculine influence we need for our development. After all, in Christ, we actually have more in common with a father-figure who is a believer than we do with a biological father who is not. There are some things our fathers would have taught us had they been there. Since they were not, we've been left to figure these things out by ourselves. This is not God's plan, since he has not left us alone. We have a church family to help us walk through life.

STEP BY STEP

Of course, when the word "family" comes up, it doesn't always bring with it warm thoughts of gathering by the fire and singing "Kumbaya." This lack of warm fuzzies may well apply both to our natural families and to our spiritual families. Families are messy, and church families are no different.

The first church I attended after becoming a believer had a lead pastor who engaged in spiritual abuse, sexual misconduct, and financial theft. At the same time, the assistant pastor committed adultery. It was a place where the pastors gave us just enough gospel so that we could know God but withheld enough so that we would be dependent upon them. They had turned what should have been a house of prayer into a house of prey. I spent six years attending there, and when I left I was running for my life. I am so thankful that I had the guts to speak up and seek outside counsel from someone who encouraged me to leave. I am also very grateful that with God's help, I never used that as an excuse to turn away from the wider church. But I wonder how many years of being exposed to this church were due to me not having the protection of and direction from a Christian father.

Many have experienced worse than I have when it comes to the church. But there are pastors and congregations who genuinely love God. After my six years of being led by a wolf in sheep's clothing, I landed in a congregational church where there was a plurality of elders, which created a healthy space for accountability. That was such a blessing and reassurance for me. Of course, that church was (and is) not perfect, but it was a beautiful pointer to my heavenly Father, and it was my striving-to-be-holy family. These elders took their responsibility as pastors seriously, and it was a balm to soothe the hurt caused by my previous church.

Truth is, God cares about his family. Of course he does— he is a perfect Father. So he warns us of those who have an appearance of godliness while seeking to do harm to the people of God by targeting the vulnerable (2 Timothy 3:1-9). And he promises to hold to account those who tempt "little ones" to sin (Luke 17:2). God cares about those of us who are fatherless because we can be particularly disposed to be taken advantage of: we often tip-toe into churches, already fighting against our own hurt, abandonment, and fears, thirsting to belong but not quite knowing how to. Those who have been burned by a church that did not act as a godly family can know with certainty that, even if there seems to be no consequence for the wrong they have endured, God will repay.

WHAT'S HAPPENING?!

What do you do when the family of God has also left you with trauma, abandonment, and pain? As well as taking some time to process the pain and heal, you need to not give up on regularly meeting with, benefiting from, and being loved by God's people. Many times it is people who cause the greatest hurt to us. Yet at the same time it is so often people that are the tools used by God for our restoration.

I often think of a friend of mine who went through three different traumatic scenarios with three different churches back to back. To start with, she was a part of a church that was steeped in legalism, so she left that church—and landed in one which taught the error of sinless perfectionism. After that she wound up in the church I attended, which contained that toxic combination of gospel teaching with spiritual abuse and secret immorality. By God's grace, she did not give up. She is still attending church and walking with the Lord today. She found a church that is godly and healthy, and that encourages her love for God and the family of God. She wrestled through all of that hurt and disappointment and she never gave up, because her hope was ultimately in God.

We are not called to stay put in an abusive, immoral, or unsound church. We are called to keep looking until we can find people seeking to reflect God by loving and faithfully preaching his word, living holy lives in view of God's truth, and loving their neighbors. There are genuine Christians who are serving the Lord, and we must find them, since we are their spiritual siblings. Not only will they be used in our lives to build us up, but we will be used in theirs to build them up. These believers can serve as spiritual mothers or fathers to those of us who are grappling with the absence of our natural family. In turn we will serve as spiritual mothers, fathers, or siblings to them.

And so we don't give up. Finding God as our Father means we can find family in a church. We find our family, and we love them and are loved by them all the way to heaven.

DAYS OF OUR LIVES
Back to my wedding day—or rather the days and months after. Once we were married, it was time to begin to apply what had until then been theoretical. I had to learn to make room for my new husband. I found that hard. Being raised by a single mom, combined with the countless times when I had had to take care of myself, had left me quite independent. I believed if anything needed to get done, I could do it, because coming up I'd had to.

In our first year of marriage we lived in a tiny basement apartment in D.C. That first year, although the Lord gave us much grace and enjoyment in marriage, it would be fair to say there were also conflicts.

One area that was particularly hard for me to shake my independence from was finances. Before we married and again as newly-weds, we had sat down and talked to other church members about money: how to set a budget, raise our credit score, and invest. Shai asked other men to walk him through what his father didn't teach him. But still, now we had to learn to live as a couple, and I was used to making my own money. I had received my first check from that Pizza Hut commercial when I was 13, and my mother had allowed me to spend the money how I wanted. Among other things, I bought for myself and a friend new outfits from Forever 21. My whole life, I had been used to determining what I would do with my money and spending it on what I felt like I deserved. Now, though, it was not my money but *our* money. For the first time since pre-marital counseling, Shai and I were sitting down to discuss a budget, which meant I couldn't just spend money like I wanted. This was hard for me. I was both frustrated by it and grateful for it. My husband was considering my leanings towards covetousness, yet it was hard as the Lord used our budgeting conversations to pry my independence away.

It wasn't only the finances. When I was in Los Angeles, I had loved taking public transportation to Hermosa Beach or Malibu. I would sometimes walk the beach for hours, rolling my jeans and squishing my toes in the wet sand as I listened to the waves strike the shore like a soothing thunder. I would wear a heavy sweater and watch the moon sometimes until midnight. A few times, I walked the two hours home. When I got married, although there was no beach in sight (unfortunately), I naturally wanted to take public transportation late at night. Shai said he didn't want me to. I felt he was impinging on my freedom. He felt he was lovingly protecting me. And he was, but it took me time to see it. (I sometimes think back to those late-night beach trips, and I praise God he kept me safe.) Again, having the care of a husband was new.

We stayed in D.C. for a few years. Part of the reason for that was because we wanted to live around godly examples of marriage, who could help us understand how to have a marriage neither of us had seen as children—a healthy marriage that could honor God and that would endure. We decided to intentionally connect with several married couples, as well single brothers and sisters in Christ. God used the church to help us love each other.

IN LIVING COLOR

Often when we think of discipleship, we limit it to reading the Bible together, discussing spiritual things, and prayer. And all those things are great! But Jesus deals with our full person. As we walk out our faith alongside others, we should be able to talk about, and receive and give counsel on, all areas of life. Part of this means asking, and being ready to answer, probing questions about how a brother or sister's past family life impacts them today, for better and for worse.

This means that when an older Christian intentionally engages with someone as a spiritual son or daughter, they should be thinking beyond "spiritual things," even though that is vital. They must also be thinking through mental, emotional and physical health, and practical wisdom. I remember how, after we had our first child, a mother in the faith came over to help me as I struggled with baby blues and nursing. My introduction to motherhood was hard, and my own mother was the breadth of the US away and wasn't there to walk me through it. But a mother in the faith was. I remember asking my single sisters for advice on child-rearing. I wanted to bring them in and let them know that I valued their counsel just as much as that of those who had children. I took walks with a sister who was informally mentoring me. We talked about marriage, motherhood, and a biblical view of the body, and it encouraged me. God was using the church in many different ways to shape my marriage, my child-rearing, and me.

Now, some years on, I have some opportunities to mentor others and talk though their mental, physical, emotional, and spiritual health. My prayer is that these sisters walk away loving Jesus more as a result of our time together, so that they can thrive in life. I have been able to help sisters recognize signs of weariness and anxiety, and be willing to ask for help when needed. I've come to see that the desire to be in control or the tendency to perfectionism is not just a burden for those who were raised in single-parent homes. It can wiggle its way into many hearts, even of those who always had their biological dad around.

All of this and more comes as a result of us taking the time to be known by others and taking the time to get to know others well. It is too easy to react and give advice out of our own assumptions. I remember a friend who shared with a brother in Christ about how she had to leave school for lack of money. His response was, "Well, why didn't you ask your dad to cover the cost?" Count the assumptions he was making in those eleven words! Not everyone has a father in their life. Not everyone has a father who has the money to help them out.

I believe this is one of the benefits of a diverse church: the greater the range of experiences, the more opportunities there are to help one another, and the richer the discipleship. Walking through life with believers whose stories are very different than mine ensures that in my decisions and hopes and dreams I am worshiping Christ and loving my neighbor who may be different than me. All this takes time. A healthy church is willing to give it. It's what we see in the very first New Testament church:

> "All who believed were together and had all things in
> common. And they were selling their possessions and
> belongings and distributing the proceeds to all, as
> any had need. And day by day, attending the temple

together and breaking bread in their homes, they
received their food with glad and generous hearts,
praising God and having favor with all the people.
And the Lord added to their number day by day those
who were being saved." (Acts 2:44-47)

Those who had more gave up some of what they had to
help those who had little. They broke bread together in their
homes. They were family. What would things look like if each
of our churches took on this mindset, sharing what we have
to help others thrive in Christ and life? We could completely
transform the next generation. Men and women who didn't
grow up with their fathers could be fathered by godly men
in the church. Single men and women would have vibrant
sibling relationships with each other as brothers and sisters in
Christ, without the awkwardness they often feel around one
another. Newly married couples who have never seen marriage
up close could have it modeled to them and would be helped
to establish healthy habits within their own relationships.
And in turn they would be able to care for their children in a
very different kind of household. The vicious cycle of family
breakdown passing on through the generations would stop,
and be replaced by a virtuous one of loving, godly, lasting
marriages and families. That's the ripple effect that the family
of God could pray toward and love each other toward.

HIGHWAY TO HEAVEN

Truth is, our natural families were always meant to be
temporary. Our natural families are a shadow of the spiritual
family that God always had in mind for us. It is that family
with whom we will dwell, sup, and worship for all eternity
as we go to the eternal place our Brother, Jesus, has prepared
for us (John 14:2). The church is our true and better family.
It is the city on a hill. These are the new-covenant people of

God, the saints in the land, the glorious ones in whom should be our delight (Psalm 16:3). They are the ones who are there to help strengthen us and also comfort us when our natural family is as broken and cracked as arid land.

A scriptural example is found in Timothy. He learned the Scriptures from his mother Eunice and grandmother Lois (2 Timothy 1:5). We don't know whether or not he was raised in a single-parent home—it is possible that his mother was a widow or that his father was not a believer. What we do know is that it was by the influence of women in his family that Timothy was spiritually raised; and we know that Paul was a spiritual father to him, encouraging him in his gifts and trust of God. To Paul, Timothy was "my beloved child" (v 2).

This is the church's calling and every saint's privileged responsibility: to make and mentor disciples. Loving one another is not an optional extra, if we know the love of our Savior:

> "By this we know love, that he laid down his life for us,
> and we ought to lay down our lives for the brothers.
> But if anyone has the world's goods and sees his
> brother in need, yet closes his heart against him, how
> does God's love abide in him? Little children, let us
> not love in word or talk but in deed and in truth."
> (1 John 3:16-18)

That was the love I was shown by the family who gave me a room when I first moved to D.C.; by the sisters who were there for me in my first year of marriage and following, and when I had my babies; by the brothers who helped Shai to know how to be a godly husband; by countless men and women who have come alongside us. Here is the call: to accept this help by faith and also to be this kind of church member; to be helped and guided, and, as we are able, to offer help and guidance to younger siblings through modeling and mentoring.

When you find a Father in God, you find a family in his church. And all it takes is a Christian village to break the one-parent-absent-father stranglehold that can burden a child. Think of what we can do when we prioritize our spiritual families' needs. When our faith meets our works. When our church members come in contact with our love. The impact on the fatherless will be life-transforming. The impact on the future could be generation-changing.

CHAPTER 5

The Missing Piece

grandma

On June 11, 2019, Momma died. She was 96 years old. My family bought our black suits and dresses and packed our bags.

Tears streamed down my cheeks as we sat in the section reserved for family at her funeral. We listened as many approached the mic to give words about how my grandma had impacted them over the years, through her at-home prayer breakfasts, women's discipleship, prison ministry, and the boys' Sunday school class she taught for over 20 years. What a legacy. I had the privilege of reciting a poem about Momma. It was an honor to speak highly of her, since I am quite certain that my salvation and my family are a direct result of the daily prayers she echoed into her Savior's ears. Even when she was suffering with dementia, my aunt told me, Momma prayed for her grandchildren every day.

We gathered together after the service. As we did, a family member commented that someone else in our family had said, as he talked about my poem, "Lil Man's daughter is so talented."

That was way out in left field. Not because of the grief we held nor the generous compliment he had given, but because Lil Man is not my father's nickname. Dee is.

JEOPARDY

My dad, Dee, didn't come to the service because of his religious beliefs, but he met us at the family house to pay his respects a few hours after our tears had dried. He came as we were just saran-wrapping the German chocolate and pound cakes and saying goodbye to some family members as they were grabbing jackets and hats before heading home. As I talked with him and we reminisced about Momma, I interacted with him normally, but I couldn't get that comment out of my head. Who was Lil Man anyway? Why did that person suggest that he was my dad? Is the man I'm speaking to my father? My mother was not around to ask.

As my dad and I talked, I found myself closely examining my father's hands, his face, his ears. I have small ears. Were his comparably small? Internally, I was having a conversation with myself: "Blair, he doesn't resemble you at all." I stopped talking. My heartrate began to accelerate.

When my dad left, I approached my cousin's orange kitchen island, where some of my family were still putting food away. I asked a few of them about who Lil Man was. The room went silent. No one said a peep. As I asked around again, someone said that Lil Man had died when I was two or three years old. But he had several children still living.

Was this my real dad? Was my dad dead? Did I have more siblings out there? I could feel the anxiety rising up in my chest with what this could all mean. And yet there possibly was no truth to it at all. What if the person who made the comment was wrong? I asked family members if they'd ever heard that I had a different dad. No one said they had.

And then the next day, a family member told me. One time, my grandmother, Momma, had alluded to the fact that my dad might not be my dad.

What!?

I couldn't ask Momma now. But this was a second instance

of my biological father's identity being questioned. Two weeks passed, and the questions were still dripping on my mind like I was standing in a bathroom with leaky pipes overhead. The more I thought about it, the more jittery my insides became. Shai told me that I would have to have a talk with my dad about it. I finally did, and it was like letting some of the air out of a balloon. I told him the comment that had been made, and that these two incidents made me want to get a paternity test. Just to be sure.

THE TWILIGHT ZONE

I still hadn't spoken to Mother, and I figured that if the test came back positive, there would be no need to alarm her. A few months later, my dad and his wife came to visit us in Philadelphia. During their visit, Shai and I talked more about it, and his advice was to not go through with the test. "Dee has been your dad all these years: so what difference would it make?" he reasoned. Shai thought asking my dad to take a test would be hurtful. Of course, I didn't want him to be hurt either—but I had to make a decision based not only on how it would affect him but how this would affect me. So on the last day of my dad's visit I restated how I would still like to take the test. He said he would be happy to do it for me if it would settle my heart. And he added that he never doubted me being his daughter. As soon as he saw me, he said, when I was only months old, he scooped me up in his arms and he felt the same love that I felt when I first saw my firstborn for the first time.

I went to my local pharmacy and bought the swab test. We took the three cotton swabs and brushed them on the insides of our cheeks. I sealed the envelope and mailed it off. It took ten days after they received the samples to email me the results.

I see the DNA email in my inbox. I don't open it. I can't. I sit down on the couch next to Shai and tell him the results are in. I need him to do it. He scans the email for the results. He looks at me and reads the results over the sound of my heart beating like an anxious drum.

There is a 0% chance of paternity.

"Not even 20%? Not even 10? Nothing?" I hear myself saying. Wow. I let the number zero settle into my mind and heart and let out a sigh. Lil Man must be my dad. Man. I am going to have to call Dee—the man I've always called Dad—and share this with him. And I know I am going to have to call my mom to talk to her about this.

I tell Dee. He says that he is just as surprised as I am. He says that after Mother had me, because he didn't have any other children to compare me with, he took me to his mom. His mom looked at me and told him, "She's yours," and that settled it for him. He trusted his mom.

THE TALK

When my mother and I finally speak, it is a few days after the conversation with Dee. My heart is racing. Anxiety peaks as I wait to get her return call. I called her the same day I got the results, but she has taken a couple of days to get back to me, which has made me suspicious. Once we are on the phone, the first thing I do is tell her that the results verify that Dee is, in fact, not my dad—and so I want to know if she knows who my biological dad is.

"I know it's been 37 years, but do you have any idea?"

There is a thick quiet from her end.

Then she says, "I've known a long time, but I didn't know how to tell you."

Known a long time?

I try not to allow this to splinter me into hundreds of pieces.

I break the awkward silence by recounting how someone had made a comment in reference to a Lil Man at the funeral. "Is *that* my father?"

I suddenly understand the vulnerability of the little bird in the book *Are You My Mother?* I have read it to my children countless times using a lighthearted staccato as the bird asks again and again, "Are you my mother?" I've never appreciated the weight that accompanies the question when you have to ask it for real.

"Mother, Lil Man—is that my father?"

"Lil Man? No, he looks like a mix of Willow Smith and T.I. No, that's not your father. I've never had anything to do with him. He was more like a cousin to me."

So at this point I have no father.

Now the story comes out. Mother tells me that after she found out she was pregnant with me, the doctors told her she was four months along. So she worked out the dates and told my dad, Dee, that she was expecting. They were not talking, because they weren't dating at the time. She was going to abort me but did not, and then planned to give me up for adoption. Then she had me two months later and decided not to give me away. When she gave birth, she thought I was a premie—but when she asked, the nurse said that I was full-term. Instead of four months along when she found out, she had been seven months along. And she hadn't been dating Dee seven months before.

Once Mother decided to keep me, she did so without any expectation that my father would help. So there was never any follow-up conversation either with Dee, who thought he was my dad and wasn't, or the other man, who was my dad but did not know it. But then Dee ran into her on the street when I was a couple months old. As soon as he saw me, my mother said, he held me in his arms and (just as he had said) just loved me right from the beginning.

My mother says she had thought he would put two and two together and realize the timing was off. But he didn't, and she said that she didn't want to shatter the smile that was on his face as he looked at me. "It's as if your dad chose you," she said. "He chose you. I just wanted you to have a family and be loved, and he and his family loved you."

As Mother shares with me her perspective, I realize that, as hard as it is to hear and as much as I even now question if there are many more unknown truths hiding in the crevices of the facts I have been told, I do feel some understanding. I'm sure the fact that I am now a mother helps soften the hard blow. My mother had wanted me to have a dad, and here one was. She had, she says, planned to tell me who my father was in my early teens, but the information never quite made the escape from her lips, and so she'd been planning to take it to the grave.

It's quite strange now, a year later, sitting with this new information. My mother says that Dee knew. It helps me see that the times that Dee did step in were purely by choice. I thought he was generous to bring candy to my sister and cousin when I was a child. I didn't know he was voluntarily being generous to the three of us. In all of those years of doubting and questioning our relationship, I was actually being intentionally loved, accepted, and chosen by someone who knew he wasn't my biological father. Now I see that he chose to call when he didn't have to. He chose to be there to the degree that he could be. Maybe he didn't want me to grow up with a vacancy that would be far more significant than just having a blank space on a birth certificate. He knew himself what being a fatherless child tasted like; maybe he wanted to offset some of the pain he knew would pile up on my plate.

When I next spoke to my father, he reassured me of his love. He told me to tell my mother that he forgave her and didn't want her to hold any regret or shame. He told me that he would always be my dad: "We have history, and a blood test won't change that." He told me to still expect visits and the money he sends to our children each year, "because that's what a father does."

He will always be my father. But he is not my biological father.

THE REAL

Now, for the first time in my life, I saw a picture of a man I resembled. My mother texted it to me. It was like a piece to a puzzle I didn't know was misplaced. He looks like me, if I had skin the color of coffee. He is a picture of me. I am a part of him. We share the same eyes, nose, lips, and ears. And yet I know nothing about him. They say a picture is worth a thousand words, and all of mine end in question marks.

My mother got in touch with my biological dad's sister, who spoke to my dad. We both swabbed our cheeks with the white q-tips. I mailed them in like the last time, and waited on the results just to be sure.

The day the DNA results were emailed to me, I opened the email myself.

99.999% paternity.

What the resemblance in the picture had told us, the email verified beyond a doubt.

ONE ON ONE

We had our first conversation on October 7, 2019, less than four months after Momma passed. Prior to punching in the numbers, I questioned what I would say. My mind was blank but I dialed anyway. Similar to my conversation with Dee at 18, when I took the plunge to have that hard conversation, I knew I couldn't wait and let fear creep in. I had to just dive into the pool of vulnerability. I figured I'd deal with the repercussions later. I dialed the number, but no one answered. I immediately called a second time. I heard, "Hello?"

"Hello..." I said. (What else do you say?)

I told him who I was, and he said, "Oh, I thought you were a bill collector," and let out a big chuckle. That broke the ice. Having your first conversation with a parent when you're an adult is strange. I felt like I'd been thrust inside one of the many Maury talk show paternity episodes I had binged on as a young teen back in the nineties. Now it was me telling someone, "You are the father." Life is a trip.

I honestly felt like this was a lot on me. I was the one who had had the truth kept from me; whose world had lurched. And I was the one doing all the calling and telling and explaining and swabbing. It was a lot. But I had signed up for it when I decided that I wanted to know the truth.

A few weeks later, my mom flipped on me about something petty, and I went from understanding to anger. The numbing shock of it all melted away, and I began to wrestle with the fact that she had lied to me my whole life. Even if she felt that she had a reason to bottle up this secret, it still hurt. Why do people protect secrets in a gilded cage like a beast restrained with embroidered bars? Embarking on this sort of deceit enables a swanky facade but eats away at life as it shackles a person to their clandestine fraudulence.

So here we are, a year on as I write, and I am still walking through the very real effects of all of this new information. I am grappling with how to establish a relationship with the father I have found at this point of my life—or with whether I should even try to. There's no playbook for this. But through it all, I have started to be able to see what has anchored my soul through this period of uncertainty and upset. Three things have helped me in this season.

THE MOMENT OF TRUTH

I have chosen to rest in the sovereignty of God, and it is here that I have found the greatest comfort. The fact that none of this caught God biting his nails in shock is my bulwark when betrayal and bitterness—those conjoined twins—try to use my hurt as a way to lure my heart away from my faith. God is in control of my book, and this is how he chose to have my chapters unfold. He has pieced together my story for his glory. I started jotting down ideas for this book on fatherlessness around six years ago. I thought that my story of finding my father was complete then, since I had found my heavenly Father and found family in his people. Little did I know that this chapter would be part of it; but he knew there was more to the story. I just needed to catch up.

I have prayed that this chapter may be here to help someone who has gone through something similar. Maybe that someone is you. With DNA kits at our fingertips, some of our stories will change—but when they do, we must never forget that our heavenly Father's unchanging nature will hold us fast.

As I process my new reality, one thing I want to make sure of is that I don't brush past this major life change and say I am ok with it all. I said earlier that we are not to be actors. I do not have to pretend to be ok—with God, it is ok to not be ok. It's ok to be angry about a 37-year-old secret kept from me which disconnects me from who I am in the flesh; or angry about the withholding of information that is rightly mine to possess. From the start of this chapter of my life, I have wanted to be honest about how I felt while at the same time not being led by my fears. I wanted to be able to be angry while being sure not to be sinning against God in that emotion. I wanted to be able to be sad and at the same time look to God for the ability to rejoice. Isn't that the Christian life? We live in the tension between the groaning caused by the realities of this fallen world and a hope based upon the realities of the life to come. I have to take those feelings and fears to God and learn to cast them over to him, being as honest as I can. I am not going to be bound by the secrets of my parents. I am determined to live free, like a sparrow the Lord watches.

"Are not two sparrows sold for a penny? And not one
of them will fall to the ground apart from your Father.
But even the hairs of your head are all numbered.
Fear not, therefore; you are of more value than many
sparrows." (Matthew 10:29-31)

A sparrow is quite insignificant. In Jesus' day, they clearly cost the equivalent of less than a cent. Yet still our Father monitors their coming and going and falling. We are God's children. We hold intrinsic value as bearers of his image and as daughters and sons of God. He cares for us and watches over us. So no matter what life brings, even if we should fall, we do not have to fear, because of him whose eyes are always upon us. When we realize he is orchestrating our entire life, we can say with David:

"O LORD, you have searched me and known me!
You know when I sit down and when I rise up;
you discern my thoughts from afar.
You search out my path and my lying down
and are acquainted with all my ways." (Psalm 139:1-3)

He is acquainted with all of our ways. We can take a deep breath and trust him rather than be crippled by things that make us afraid.

ONE DAY AT A TIME

One of the things the gospel helps me to do is to forgive. I remember having a conversation with my dad Dee about my mom and how hurt I was about it all. He asked me, matter of factly, "But you forgive her, don't you?" "Of course I do," I replied. After I hung up, I prayed to God: "Lord, have I truly forgiven her?" I wanted to be honest before God with how I felt. It is easy to say I forgive my mom, but I want to truly do so. I have been asking God not to allow any bitter root to spring up within me. There are five things I have done and am continuing to do in order to make sure that I am living out the forgiveness which has been so richly lavished upon me.

1. Pray for my Parents

In the Sermon on the Mount, we are called to love and pray for our enemies, as children of the God who has loved us even when we were his enemies (Matthew 5:43-48). Not many of us have enemies as parents. They may let us down badly, but few of them act in enmity toward us. But if we are called to pray for our enemies, certainly we should pray for our parents, however hurt we are. I have tried to commit to praying for my parents (all three of them) as often as they come to mind.

In loving those who have hurt us and in praying for those who have misused us, we show ourselves to be true children of our Father in heaven. If our parents are near, we often know their struggles and can pray for their salvation and deliverance from sin and trauma.

2. Seek Accountability

I do not try to battle these difficult feelings alone. I need to allow other trustworthy, godly siblings (peers) to know what is happening in my heart. I have asked them to hold me accountable and regularly ask me how I'm processing all that has happened. I have asked them to keep me in prayer so that I do not give in to bitterness or unforgiveness.

3. Write the Story Down

I journal. I have taken the time to write down my story so that I can have a chance to process what's happened. (Some of it became this book…) I have given myself permission to be transparent and raw with my feelings. As I have done this on paper, I have been able to wrestle with God in my hurt and disappointment. I have learned to try not to judge my thoughts straight away, but just to get them down.

Sometimes we have questions that we have never asked. What questions do you have for your father? What would you like to know? Write it down. Even if circumstances do not allow us to ever ask these questions to him personally, jotting them down helps us to face them and to pray through them.

4. Seek out a Biblical Counselor or Therapist

The trauma of fatherlessness wiggles its way into other areas of life. It shows up in anxiety, depression, an inability to express emotions, and struggles with sin. You may find that you are having a difficult time processing and that it's affecting your day-to-day relationships. That's what counselors are there to help us navigate. As helpful as our spiritual family may be, there are times when we need to outsource to someone who is trained to help us get at the root of what is going on. Thankfully, we are having more conversations about mental health in the church these days, causing us to take away the stigma associated with it. We are whole beings, made in the image of God. God cares about every bit of us. He cares about our spiritual health and our emotional, physical, and mental health too.

I needed help this past year, from an expert.

5. Meditate upon Forgiveness

The parable of the unmerciful servant in Matthew 18 is there for the moments when we have been greatly sinned against and are struggling to forgive. When I owed God a monumental amount of debt, he forgave me. So far be it from me to choke out the one who owes me, but owes me so much less. Jesus does not minimize the way you or I have been sinned against. But he does help me to understand that I have sinned against God far, far more than I have been sinned against in this situation. The fact that another sinner has sinned against me is hard to grapple with, but when I see it in light of my monumental debt before our holy God, and when I meditate on how he has pardoned me in a way that is free to me though so costly for him, it helps me to forgive. The one who has been forgiven much loves much.

I want to consider what the biblical call to forgive as we have been forgiven means, and what it *doesn't* mean. It means that we give the offense and the hurt that came with that offense over to God, committing never to throw it back up in the face of the one who wronged us, and never to replay it to ourselves or to others. It means that we genuinely cast it over to God. When the thought of the offense comes back up, we give it back over to him and wash, rinse, and repeat. That is what forgiveness means. What it does not mean is that if being around a parent or anyone else would somehow put you in danger, you have to pretend that it's a safe place for you. Sometimes forgiveness looks like loving someone from a distance for the sake of physical safety or mental health. It may mean putting some boundaries in place to assist that relationship. A wise pastor or counselor can help figure out what wisdom looks like.

Forgiveness is not always instantaneous, especially if that person is still hurting us day after day or is refusing to acknowledge the hurt they have inflicted. In that case it is a fight to live out the Scriptures. If forgiveness does not seem to come immediately, we must beg God for a supernatural work to happen in our heart.

One helpful tip is to list out the specific offenses caused by your parents and ask God to help you to forgive each item on the list. Sometimes when we approach forgiveness by thinking about one hazy clump of sins, it's easy to get caught off guard when offenses rise back up, because we haven't truly considered the specificity of the offense until we are hurt again by it—and then it's too late because we are already responding with anger or bitterness.

Forgiveness is not easy; but it is still necessary. God is not asking us to do anything that he doesn't already do toward us. He always gives us more grace (James 4:6)—and that includes the grace to change us to enable us to forgive. What he is calling us to do is something we cannot do on our own. We need the Holy Spirit's help, and we have it.

Unforgiveness does not just corrode relationships. It eats away at our hearts. There is a saying that "holding on to unforgiveness is like drinking poison and waiting on the other person to die." Our Christian life depends upon us forgiving others. Jesus forgave those who murdered him and entrusted himself to the one who judges justly, without retaliation (1 Peter 2:19-23)—and we are called to follow in his steps. And so I honestly consider what I have been forgiven of, and I honestly consider what I am called to forgive, and I pray, "Lord, help me to love and forgive my mom like you have loved and forgiven me."

THIS IS US

Lastly, I am realizing that truth is what will heal the consequences of my fatherlessness. The only way to be made whole is to realize that the gospel is able to turn the pain inside out, to help me look at the wound and trace it to the source. I can acknowledge all the pain I feel. The pain may be too powerful for me, but it's not too powerful for God.

He says to cast my cares upon him—and he doesn't say only to cast the dainty ones. God can deal with the mountains that need to be moved. There is a sufficient prescription for tackling any crusted-over wounds left as absent-father debris, and that is to cling to Psalm 27:10: "Though my father and mother forsake me, the LORD will receive me" (NIV).

A fatherless child possesses no wound that our heavenly Father has not promised to mend. He will receive us. The question is not "Can he heal?" but "Do you want to be healed?" That is what Jesus asked a man who had been physically paralyzed for 38 years, the age I am as I write this (John 5:6). It sounds like a strange question—but a wound can become so much a part of us that we cannot imagine parting with it. In a way, fatherlessness can be paralyzing. It becomes part of our identity. It winds itself into our history and our present. I have to come to Jesus and say, "YES! Yes. I'm ready to be healed. Yes, I will not allow my natural circumstances to get in the way of me living the abundant, God-honoring life you have for me." Being paralyzed by natural circumstances is neither necessary nor right, since God cares for the birds and cares for us much more than them. God is able to set us free from whatever hinders us. This does not mean that he will necessarily give us that picture-perfect family we may have in mind. But it does mean that he gives us freedom from being hindered by the family that has wounded us, that he gives us a new family in his people, and that he gives us himself as our Father.

2019 was the year I discovered I had three fathers. The one I didn't know much coming up, who now I see chose to love me; the one I didn't even know existed coming up, whose DNA I share; and the one in heaven, who chose to love me perfectly before the creation of the world, and who has overseen every detail of each chapter of my life. What do I do with all of this? By God's grace I have committed to pray for my parents, to seek accountability, to journal my thoughts, to seek out a counselor when it feels like too much to handle on my own, to meditate upon forgiveness… and lastly, to hold on to the promises of God that I find in his word. These promises are precious when life is tipped upside down. So I cling to him, remembering that his Son says, "In the world you will have tribulation. But take heart; I have overcome the world" (John 16:33).

I choose to put my faith in the one who has overcome this world. He overcame this world through the power of the Spirit and obeying the will of his Father. I am united with him. He is the missing piece of the fatherless puzzle. He condescends, loves, cares for, and even dies for his brothers and sisters, who are sons and daughters of his Father—empowering them, by faith, to overcome this world too.

CHAPTER 6

#GirlDad

"**G**irls are the best. I would have five more girls if I could. I'm a girl dad."

Kobe Bryant was being interviewed by ESPN when he mentioned how much he loved being a dad to daughters. The dedication Kobe showed towards his daughters was evident in him coaching their basketball games and, prior to retirement, taking a helicopter from practice to his home to avoid traffic so that he would make it in time to be able to pick them up from school.

Since his shocking death in 2020, #GirlDad has trended on twitter in his memory. We feel saddened for Kobe's daughters, who no longer have their father with them to watch them blossom into women. We look at these posts in honor of him and other fathers like him, and they make us ooh, ahh, and shed tears at these fathers who love their daughters unashamedly. It is wonderful to see men boldly display their love by plaiting and swooping baby hair, mastering the pirouette, attending their girls' soccer games, and gladly playing make-believe over pink cups of imaginary tea.

Many of us look at these #GirlDads and wonder what could have been had we had a dad who loved us in such a way. What would it have been like to receive this type of affirmation from our fathers? What would it have been like to have a #GirlDad?

Around one out of four women identify as fatherless. While the presence or absence of fathers tends to be assessed by how it impacts boys, the connection between a father and daughter is special and, surely, no less crucial, since God did not set up this creation so that a parent was particularly significant only for children of the same gender as themselves. Fathers are vital to a daughter's development. They have a lasting impact on her self-image and future relationships, and on her emotional, physical, and spiritual health.

A father can have a serious negative impact while living in the home—he has the power to provoke and discourage his kids (Colossians 3:21). But, as we have seen, his absence will be just as powerful. Yet there is often a subconscious assumption that as long as she has her mother, a daughter will bypass any dysfunction and arise from her dad-less childhood unscathed. It really shows how little value we place upon fatherhood.

Truth is, we fatherless daughters are hurting just as much as fatherless sons. We feel the effects of our fathers' spiritual, emotional, and physical ghosting. But the more common the broken bond is, the more comfortable it is to ignore it. I don't see many Christians asking the questions, "How does fatherlessness affect women?" "How can we address this issue and care well for our sisters?"

I have talked already about some of my own struggles with identity while growing up. Not having a father created a hole which the father of lies tried to fill. Ultimately, if we do not have God as our Father, we will have the devil. That is stark, but those are Jesus' words. Those who "cannot bear to hear my word," he says, "are of your father the devil, and your will is to do your father's desires" (John 8:43-44). Satan is in the wings, unseen but making every effort to influence us by manipulating us and using our desires against us. When it comes to our spiritual life, fatherlessness is not an option; it is God or the evil one.

And if it is God, the devil still does not give up. He remains a roaring lion seeking to devour us by deceiving us into falling away from the truth (1 Peter 5:8). His time is short but his teeth are sharp. So what are the lies that this father of lies tries to whisper into the head and heart of the woman whose earthly father is physically, emotionally or spiritually absent? How does the devil seek to entice us to run into his deathly arms?

I want to consider two main lies. First, that there's something wrong with you. And second, that there's something wrong with men.

LIE #1: THERE'S SOMETHING WRONG WITH YOU

Those of us who grew up without the unconditional presence and love of a father find it tempting to make an idol of attention, be a people-pleaser, and live constantly in search of love.

Idolizing Attention

Idolatry in this context is when we seek validation, security, or meaning from the attention we can receive from someone other than God. It's when we become lovers of ourselves and arrogant (2 Timothy 3:1-2), making ourselves the focus of our lives rather than God. Prior to coming to the Lord, I wanted the attention on me. When I got dressed in the morning, I would think, "What will get me the most attention?" I wasn't scantily clad, but I was aiming to draw eyes toward me. In my senior yearbook I was chosen as "the most likely to stand out in a crowd." I would wear wooden clogs or bright mixed matched shoes and braids brushing my ankles in order to get people's attention. Getting that was the highlight for me.

There is nothing wrong with dressing up or having style. But we must consider the motives for why we are making the choices we do. This doesn't mean godliness looks like camouflaging ourselves like a cuttlefish in the sand, hoping to go completely unnoticed by everyone. It means we place more weight upon internal than outer adornment, we care more about God's attention than that of others, and therefore we value what God values rather than what those around us do. We would rather God smiled on us than that everyone else smiled at us.

Alongside how we dress, we can seek out attention in what we say. It is easy to make every conversation about us. Rather than rest in our God-given identity, we want to somehow convince people that we are worthy by showing off our wealth, intelligence, education, talents, or connections. It's an attempt to have others think more highly of us. The things we say may be true, but we are not called to boast in our accomplishments. I love how Paul reminds us to consider the truth that we're not that dope. Truth is, I am not that wise, powerful, or high-born, and that's ok, because the Lord is the one I can and should boast in (1 Corinthians 1:26-31). He gives us our value.

Attention can be sought not only from those around us but from those who come from us. A child seems like the ultimate attention-giver that we so desire. After all, a young child will look to you for everything (even when you are trying to sleep). But looking for someone outside of the Lord to fulfill your desires for attention always ends poorly. A child cannot satiate the longings of your heart, which the Lord alone can satisfy. That is a weight no child can bear, and it will crush them. Children are to be loved, not worshiped.

Each of these bids for attention is because we believe the lie that something is wrong with us that means that people won't love us or appreciate us for who we are, so we have to highlight or embellish something about ourselves in order to be accepted or valued. We believe that the answer is found apart from God. The best way to fight an infernal lie is with heavenly truth, so here it is: <u>God says you are accepted on the basis of his grace rather than anything you do or have. He loves you because he loves you, and his eyes are on you because he loves you</u>.

The "Perfect" People-Pleaser

My parents broke off their relationship prior to my birth, and there was never a conversation to explain to me why that was the case. Although I didn't think that the reason they weren't together was me, I assumed that the reason why my dad Dee was not in my life was that he didn't want to be near me. Though I now know that wasn't true, it was a heavy load to carry growing up.

When kids don't have these conversations with an adult, they navel-gaze and try to figure things out themselves. We self-analyze, concluding that our father's absence must be the result of our sins of commission or omission. As we get older, this often works itself out as a belief that we need to be accepted or loved, and so we will do anything to please. We spin ourselves into a web of impossible expectations anchored in perfectionism. After all, if we were perfect, people would stick around with us, wouldn't they?

So we ask the question, "What's wrong with *me*?" Or "What did I do to cause my dad to leave? What can I do to fix it and make my dad come back?" This shame-blame game never leads to true healing, but only more brokenness. When we look within and blame ourselves for the reason daddy left or isn't near, we live our entire lives doubting. We doubt our God-given worth and trade it in for being a people-pleaser.

Truth is, the woman who grew up with her father in the home did not have him because of some intrinsic virtue within herself. She was not more lovable than us, nor was she without flaws. The flip side is that growing up without a father is not the result of some sin we have committed at birth or during our childhood. When we blame ourselves for choices our fathers have made, we preach to ourselves a dangerous lie that says, "If only I can have everything together, then men will stay in my life." We tell ourselves, "I must be the perfect daughter, the perfect friend, the perfect student, the perfect wife, in order to avoid abandonment."

The woman who believes this lie places herself in the center, ultimately believing that every relationship rests upon her. But the center is reserved for God's throne. We cannot force anyone to stay in our life. Genuine loving relationships cannot be manipulated. All relationships require faith. We trust the Lord by not taking responsibility for something that is no guilt of our own. We trust the Lord by holding others accountable for what they are called to do. I can only be, and could only ever be, a daughter. My responsibility as a daughter is not to try to make my father father me.

Perfection is an impossible standard to place on ourselves and on others. It constructs unattainable expectations for us and other sinners, setting up ourselves and them for failure. Jesus is not looking for the perfect woman to call his sister. If that were the case, he would never have chosen any of us. He knows we are imperfect and he still says, *I want to have a relationship with you.* He knows that we will consistently fail and so he says, *I'm going to do the perfect work required to pull you out of your slavery to the prince of the darkness and into a relationship with me.*

Jesus, the sinless one, came to save sinners. It is not a perfect woman whom Scripture says is to be praised, but a woman who fears the Lord (Proverbs 31:30). The woman who is honest enough about herself to know she needs to be forgiven much is the woman who is free to love much. When we know we are secure in the love of God because of his grace, we don't live to please others—rather, we are freed up in order to love others.

In Search of Love

If the first man to tell you "I love you" is not your father—
or if your father said those words while his actions stated
otherwise—it is easy to search for those words and the
feelings they produce from another man or source. There's
tragic truth in the saying, "Men give love to get sex, and
women give sex to receive love." How many women have
mistaken sexual intercourse for love? We rationalize by
saying, "He said he likes me. He shows me attention. When
he holds me, I feel like I'm worth something." The craving
to be desired, and the confusion of being desired with being
loved, makes it all too easy for a woman to be tricked into
using her body as collateral.

The truth is, if a man is asking you to compromise your
walk with the Lord to indulge in sexual immorality, he is not
showing trust in God or love for you as his sister. And if you
are initiating sexual immorality to get love or anything else,
then you are not showing that you trust God or love your
brother. Giving ourselves up physically or emotionally to a
man without a covenant is a carrot-chase, just like it was in
Eden when the devil used fruit and told the first woman, "If
you eat of that fruit, you will not surely die." Today he dangles
a carrot with a message which says, "Unless you give up your
body, you will surely not be loved." He waves the promise of
being loved in front of us, but behind it is immorality, lust,
and heartbreak. We think that we're being led toward a man
who will love us, when in reality he is a mere cover for Satan,
who wants to destroy us.

In his book *The Reason for God*, Tim Keller gives this
definition of sin:

> "Sin is the despairing refusal to find your deepest
> identity in your relationship and service to God. Sin
> is seeking to become oneself, to get an identity, apart

from him … So, according to the Bible, the primary way to define sin is not just the doing of bad things, but the making of good things into *ultimate* things."[15]

Being intimately loved by a man is a good thing. Sex inside the covenant of marriage is a good thing. But these are not ultimate things. God's ways are good. God's commands are good. There is a reason why sex is reserved for marriage. There is purpose in not awakening love until it is time (Song of Solomon 8:4). If God is withholding these good (yet not ultimate) things from us, it is for a good reason which we might not currently comprehend. Growing up without a man who showed us love does not make it ok to chase that love wherever and however we see fit. That way will not lead us to the love we seek. That type of love comes from God, who knows everything about us, can be trusted to do what is good for us, and is committed to loving us.

LIE #2: THERE'S SOMETHING WRONG WITH MEN
Before my relationship with Shai, I was what you would call "militant" in my singleness. Just to be clear, singleness is wonderful, not second best (1 Corinthians 7:6-8). There is no need to apologize for choosing to be single, or for being content with being single even if that is not your first choice. But the problem with my militancy was what lay behind it: fear.

When Shai first told me he was interested in courting me, we'd been friends for around nine months. To be honest, the word "courting" made me feel my lack of a godly father. After all, the way people talk about "courting" mostly assumes firstly that you have your father in your life and secondly, that he will be interested in meeting with your prospective mate. I did not feel that I had that. So I had my pastor step in to ask

---

15 *The Reason for God* (Penguin, 2008), p 162.

Shai the hard questions for me. (After I was married, my dad Dee expressed how he would have liked to have been a part of the process. I thought it was only for Christian dads, since that's what all of the courting books said. In retrospect, I wish I had included him.) Once Shai passed those series of "tests" from my pastor, he invited me to have ice cream at Baskin-Robbins, and shared the reasons why he was interested in pursuing a relationship with me. I did not respond in the way Shai was hoping, nor the way they do in the movies. When Shai retells this story, he says I shot him down. Truth is, I did. Bottom line is, I freaked out.

"What if the Lord wants me to be single?" I asked him with tears in my eyes. I still remember Shai's face. He suggested that we pull back completely and take the idea of a relationship off the table. So we did. Shai got on his plane for a six-hour flight back home from California, and I went back to my dorm. For the next two weeks it seemed that, just about everywhere I went, I heard about marriage. As I prayed, the Lord exposed the truth: my words were me trying to protect myself from my own fears. I was afraid of marriage in part because of some of the lies I believed about men. All of the things I had heard about getting married and how your husband turns into a monster once the honeymoon is done were roaming around in my mind. I had been traveling each weekend, sharing poetry, my testimony, and the gospel. I was fearful that I'd go from ministering poetry on stage in front of a receptive crowd to being at home changing diapers. The thought of potentially being a mother put a knife to the neck of any lingering fantasies of "Christian greatness" in public ministry.

But what I realized was that I had the freedom to choose. I could remain single or choose to head towards the direction of marriage, but what I must not do was live in fear and let that fear dictate my choice. I had to walk by faith.

The more I thought about it, I also started to miss my friendship with Shai. Honestly, there was no reason to not take a step of faith and move forward. There were no red flags or concerns that I had regarding him. I had to allow God to knock down the walls that had been built by years of fatherlessness, trauma, fear, and lies. I had to live by faith.

WHAT-IFS

If the only marriage you've seen close up is a broken one, and all you saw of men as you grew up was them leaving or cheating or hurting, then it's natural to be fearful of the idea of marriage and the idea of living with a man. Yet God's word says that "marriage should be honored by all" (Hebrews 13:4, NIV). We can't honor and love what we fear. We have to trust God that a marriage with him in it and over it is different than what we have so far seen. Don't get me wrong: we are in a fallen world, and there are a lot of reasons to be tempted to fear. However, we have an opportunity to gain victory over this world. And marriage might be one place where we do it.

The crazy thing is, our culture encourages this distrust. So we jump up and bob our heads to "All my ladies who are independent, throw yo hands up at me." We are taught that we don't need anybody. We feed ourselves words from the "gospel" song, "As long as I got King Jesus, I don't need nobody else." Truth is, we can't do it on our own. It's not good for man to be alone. God has made us to live and thrive in community. Singleness is a beautiful thing when you do it in faith. But if you are single because you are living in fear, it is time to ask God for deliverance. This does not mean that the Lord will automatically give you a spouse. What it does mean is that even if the Lord has singleness in his plan for you, you can live your life trusting God in your singleness and at the same time having a high view of marriage.

The command to not fear comes more often than any other command in the Bible. Faith brings freedom where once there was fear. Faith proclaims gospel truth that chases away the devil's whispered lies. God will be with us. God will never forsake us. We can be free from worry, because Christ died and rose again and he says to give up our burdens to him! We can be free from anxiety, because Christ died and rose again and he says we can cast our cares on him! We can be free from our past, no matter how dark it is, because Christ died and rose again and he says that "if anyone is in Christ, he is a new creation. The old has passed away; behold, the new has come" (2 Corinthians 5:17).

What does this mean practically? It means we can triumph over the what-if questions that our fears prompt and promote.

In fear we say, "What if I never get married because of my issues or my past?" In faith we can say, "How might God use my situation to bring glory to his name? Maybe someone else can benefit from hearing my story and seeing how God can transform what may seem like the most unlikely woman into a woman who is united to Christ, the bridegroom."

In fear we say, "What if my husband leaves me like my dad left my mom?" In faith we can believe the best about our husband. Love believes all things and hopes all things. Love doesn't expect the worst or mark our spouse out to likely be guilty simply because our minds have said that it is so. One of the best pieces of advice we received in premarital counseling was when our pastor encouraged us to never throw out the "d" word when we argued. That word so easily rolls off the tongue, and not only when there has been some heinous sin like adultery or abandonment, which the Bible recognizes may be times to mention divorce (although forgiveness and reconciliation may yet win the day), but also just because two people seem to hit an impasse. Our relationships do not need to mirror those of our parents.

My prayer is that when conflict arises in my house, the word "divorce" will never be uttered. Marriage requires grace. As women we have heard, and perhaps our experience has told us, that there are no good men out there and that all men cheat. That does something to our psyche. The world says assume the worst. The gospel says assume the best. I am not suggesting we be naive, but rather that we be godly. Because of the gospel, we can know that there are good men: men who, yes, are sinners and are not perfect, but who fear the Lord and take their marriage covenant seriously. Because of the gospel, we can work through our conflicts, leaving a legacy of devotion rather than divorce.

In fear we say, "What if I push my husband away like my mom did my dad?" It is, of course, easier to repeat the sins of our parents than to look like our heavenly Father. If we do nothing, we will most likely be conformed to the image of those we were around. (I will share more about this in chapter 8.) It is not enough to say, "I don't want to be like the person who's had a harmful influence on me." But we can do something about this. We can do what Scripture says and actually allow the gospel to do its good work in our lives, by putting off our old behaviors and putting on the new virtues that we have access to because of the Spirit who lives in us.

For example, if you watched your mother make degrading, disrespectful, or emasculating remarks to your father, then it is not enough to simply say, "I don't want to do that." What we must do is see our tendency towards it, we must call it what the Bible calls it—corrupting talk that tears others down—and we must repent. We must memorize what God says: "Let no corrupting talk come out of your mouths, but only such as is good for building up, as fits the occasion, that it may give grace to those who hear" (Ephesians 4:29). And we must pray, asking the Holy Spirit to enable us to use our words to build up and edify, and to show us how we can intentionally find ways to speak life to our spouse. We must choose each day, with God's help, to build up relational capital by sowing good godly seeds into our marriage and relationships. We must resist the urge to break our husband down before he can break us down, or break his heart before he has an opportunity to break ours.

So many of us have what-ifs: those questions that fear leaves in our minds as a result of the devil's lie that there's something wrong with men. So we identify these questions and expose them and bring gospel truth to them. They won't like the light.

MAINTAINING A PROPER VIEW

It is not just for the sake of a potential husband or an actual husband that we need to fight the lies. It is for the sake of our relationship with God. So how can you have a proper view of yourself and others again? By pursuing honesty, healing, and honor.

1. Honesty

I pray about my hurt. The beauty of our relationship with the Lord is that we don't have to be phony. He knows anything we are going through anyways. We can take all of our concerns, fears, disappointments, worries, shame, unforgiveness, anger, and sin to him. He will go to work in us to replace those very real feelings with a holy response: loving him (Mark 12:29-31), viewing ourselves rightly (Romans 12:3), and loving even those who have hurt us (Matthew 5:44).

2. Healing

Healing requires forgiveness, and forgiveness requires prayer. We were here in previous chapters, but it needs saying again:

because we have been forgiven, we can choose to forgive others. Those who are forgiven much, love much!

Truth is, a father may not ask for forgiveness, or because of death or other circumstances he may not ever have an opportunity to. But we can still meditate upon the extent of our own sinfulness and ask God to give us a merciful heart. We can still ask God to do what we have no power in and of ourselves to do. Yet note that forgiveness is a command: forgive so that you will be forgiven (Luke 6:37; Matthew 6:14-15). Yes, your dad has sinned against you; but yes, you must forgive him. Pray that God changes your heart and (if your dad is alive) changes your dad's heart too.

1. Honor

"Honor your father" (Exodus 20:12). This does not mean we put ourselves in a position to be in harm's way. However, if there is no physical or emotional danger, and if we are (or could be) in contact with our dad, we should pray about how we might be able to encourage him.

Can you think about anything that your father did that was good? Did he give you candy as a child? Did he pay child support? Did he send you a letter? I know it's not much, but it's something. It's something to be thankful for and to honor him for.

Try to give some benefit of the doubt. Often, because our father isn't there, we can easily assume the worst about him on all fronts. We may have heard negative things from our mother, but in those things we have only heard one side of the story.

If we are able to reconcile with him, we can honestly share all the ways we are thankful for him along with what has been particularly difficult.

I know you may be in a situation where you have not experienced anything good from your father. You can't think of one single thing. Let me tell you something: *you* are his one thing. You are alive. You are the result of God's kindness to your father, because he used your father to create you. If you can't say thank you to your father for participating in your existence, turn to your heavenly Father and praise *him* for it!

Honoring men goes wider than honoring our dads as far as we are able to. We must also let God redefine the vision we have of manhood. Let God's word show you what a man should be. Let God's people show you that vision lived out. Avoid idolizing men who love their wives and lead their families—but praise God for them and learn from them.

So, we let our brothers treat us like a sister. Let them hold the door for us. Let the men in our life honor us, and honor them in return. Let them lavish us with kindness and protection.

If you are married, let your husband know that you need him. If he will hold the door for you or carry the car seat, girl, let him. Do not believe the lie of 21st-century Western culture, which says that letting a man lead and care for you will diminish your womanhood.

GOD IS A #GIRLDAD

I said higher up that some may look at #GirlDads and wonder what could have been, had we had a dad who loved us in such a way. What would it have been like to have received this type of affirmation from our fathers? What would it have been like to have had a #GirlDad?

Matter of fact is, we can know what it is like, for we do have a #GirlDad. And his impact on you can be—should be—greater than the impact an earthly father's absence or lovelessness had and has on you.

We who did not have our father around can cling to God in a special way. It's just like the person who has experienced hunger. When you don't know where your next meal is coming from, you are able to rely upon God as your Provider in a way that someone who has always had a pantry full of food does not. Here is a wonderful opportunity to meet with God in a way which would have never existed if everything had been great and gone perfectly according to our plans. Although none of us would have ever requested to grow up without a loving father, we can look at this as an opportunity to draw nearer and nearer to God to supply every need we have. When we get in a bind, we might not be able to get Dad on the phone, but our heavenly Father is right there, ready to hear our prayers and answer them according to what he knows is best for us. God is good, he gives good gifts, and he will never leave us nor forsake us. God is a #GirlDad, and we're forever his girls.

CHAPTER 7

Becoming the Dad I Never Had

BY SHAI LINNE

I think it was around the time of the third or fourth ultrasound that the feelings of fear and borderline panic began to kick in. It was not because I noticed that the baby's head was shaped like mine (poor thing!) but because at that point, what was merely theoretical in my mind crystallized into something tangible and scary. In a few short months, I would be responsible for loving, protecting, providing for, and raising up a precious little soul! The very thought was overwhelming. And I had no reference point for how to be a parent.

Of course, there was joy too. When Blair told me that she was pregnant with our eldest son, Sage, I was overjoyed. It felt surreal, like I was standing outside of myself, watching my response as I reacted to the good news. For the first few weeks, I was on cloud nine. Whatever I previously thought learning I was going to be a father for the first time would be like, this was so much better. I couldn't wait to share the news with my mom, my friends, my church, and any stranger who happened to engage me in small talk. I might as well have been skipping and whistling as I accompanied Blair to the prenatal appointments. I had long desired to be a father, and I was determined to do it the right way.

HEROES

Growing up, I heard a lot about "baby mamas" and "baby daddys," but almost nothing about wives and husbands. I not only lacked models of godly Christian marriage, but marriages of any kind were rare in my family. My mom and dad were never married. They broke up not long after I was born. In my early years, I remember my father being a regular presence in my life. I would stay with him on some weekends and talk to him on the phone from time to time. Thankfully, he wasn't abusive, on drugs, or in and out of jail like some of my friends' dads. He was wise and hardworking, had a great sense of humor, and was generally fun to be around. I enjoyed spending time with him and eagerly looked forward to each weekend visit.

As I grew older, our time together decreased. I'm not quite sure why that was—we lived within a few miles of each other for most of my childhood. When I realized that I was the one primarily initiating our interactions, resentment towards my dad began to develop in my heart. In his absence, I unconsciously sought out other older males to fill the void and show me what it meant to be a man. From childhood and into my teen years, I was on an endless quest for heroes, and I was open to finding them wherever they appeared in my life. My worldview was shaped by the rappers I listened to. My dreams and aspirations were molded by the artists, athletes, and entertainers I admired. My sense of morality was informed by cousins, uncles, and peers who lived by the code of the streets. Life for me was basically a modern-day urban iteration of the book of Judges in which we all did what was right in our own eyes (Judges 17:6). By the time I turned 18, my contact with my father was practically nonexistent, and my childhood disappointment had morphed into anger and resentment. I told myself that I wanted nothing to do with him, which, looking back, was really a reflexive defense mechanism to shield myself from the devastating knowledge that my father wanted nothing to do with me. This preemptive rage towards him accompanied me into adulthood like an overbearing chaperone, always around to place restrictions on any fleeting moments of happiness I might experience with the cruel reminder that paternal abandonment cast a deep shadow over my entire being.

TRUTH BE TOLD

I became a Christian in my twenties through reading the Gospel of John. It was very much an overnight conversion. I was running hard away from God towards eternal destruction, and he sovereignly intervened and opened my eyes to the truth of who Jesus is and what he accomplished on my behalf through his life, death, and resurrection. As I voraciously read the Bible for the first time, I began to see the world through new eyes. Through the Spirit and the word, I now had divine guidance that enabled me to interpret my life and all my experiences up to that point.

It was particularly sweet for me to learn from Scripture that God uniquely reveals himself to his people as their Father. I know that some people have trouble with relating to God as Father due to poor examples of earthly fathers. As for me, I embraced the idea wholeheartedly. Think about how the Bible describes our heavenly Father. He's holy (Isaiah 6:3). He's gracious (Psalm 116:5). He's kind (Psalm 145:17). He's just (Deuteronomy 32:4). He's merciful (Luke 6:36). He's powerful

(Psalm 106:8). He's patient (2 Peter 3:9). He's wise (Psalm 104:24). He's always present (Deuteronomy 31:6). He loves us sacrificially (Romans 8:32). He provides all of his children's needs (Philippians 4:19). He protects us (2 Timothy 4:18). He gives us good gifts (James 1:17). He delights in us for Jesus' sake (John 17:23), and he has secured our everlasting joy in His presence so that we might spend quality time with him forever (Psalm 16:11). Who wouldn't want a father like this?

Nevertheless, when I first became a Christian I saw the fatherhood of God as a metaphor: God's way of describing unfathomable heavenly realities in language we can understand. Over the years, however, I've come to understand that God didn't look at earthly fathers and say, *See! I'm like that!* Rather he created earthly fathers as a faint picture of who he is in himself. Michael Reeves picks up on this in his book *Delighting in the Trinity*:

> "Since God is, before all things, a Father, and not primarily Creator or Ruler, all his ways are beautifully fatherly. It is not that this God 'does' being Father as a day-job, only to kick back in the evenings as plain old 'God.' It is not that he has a nice blob of fatherly icing on top. He is Father. All the way down. Thus all that he does he does as Father. That is who he is. He creates as a Father and he rules as a Father; and that means the way he rules over creation is most unlike the way any other God would rule over creation."[16]

When we understand the fatherly character of God in this way, we realize that all the grace necessary to overcome the challenges of fatherlessness are available to all who trust in Christ. With that said, however, even after coming to Christ the absence of my earthly father did not stop being painful.

---

16 *Delighting in the Trinity* (IVP, 2012), p 23.

Once I learned the importance of forgiveness from the teachings of Jesus (Matthew 6:12; 18:21-35), I knew I had to forgive my dad. I felt a deep conviction that I needed to reach out to him and seek reconciliation. By that time, it had been years since we last spoke. I called him and arranged to meet with him at his house. I was very optimistic about the meeting. In fact, I played the entire scenario out in my head many times before we met: I would approach the steps to his front door in order to ring his doorbell. Before I made it up the steps, I would hear him call out to me from down the street. I would turn in his direction, and our eyes would lock. (Cue the theme music from *Chariots of Fire*. Or was it *St. Elmo's Fire?* One of those.) In slow motion, he would drop his briefcase and begin sprinting towards me like the father in the Prodigal Son parable. We would tearfully embrace, and, with his arm around me, we would walk into the house. For the next few hours, I would share how his absence caused me pain. I would be very honest about the bitterness that I felt towards him. Then I would share the hope that I have in Christ and tell him that I was ready to forgive him, forget the past, and begin a new chapter in our relationship. This expression of grace would break him into pieces. Weeping, he would beg for forgiveness, which I would eagerly grant him. He would affirm his love for me and confess how his own fear and feelings of guilt kept him from reaching out all those years. Amazed that God would transform me in this way, his next question would be, "What must I do to be saved?" I would share the gospel with him and he would accept Christ on the spot. And that day would be the first day of the rest of our lives. Happily ever after and all that.

Well, that's not how it went down. In fact, particularly after all that build-up in my mind, our meeting was anti-climactic and disappointing. He didn't have much to say. He sat quietly as I shared with him the pain of my upbringing and the joy of my conversion. When I was done, he said, "Well, my dad wasn't around when I grew up either, so... It is what it is."

And that was that.

Nothing had changed, as far as I could tell. It would be years before he and I would speak again. I had to work through forgiving him without his acknowledging any wrongdoing. Thankfully, growing in my understanding of the gospel has helped the bitterness I once felt to dissipate. I don't know if we'll ever have the relationship that I desired. We certainly don't yet. I eventually had to give it over to the Lord, trusting his providence and gaining new appreciation for his perfect fatherhood.

ARRESTED DEVELOPMENT

As I sought to navigate life as an adult convert, I discovered that there were still many things that I had to learn on my own because I hadn't learned them from my dad. By God's grace, I was able to understand and articulate theology, but I was playing catch-up when it came to basic, mundane, nitty-gritty kinds of things like how to take care of a car, how to think about home ownership, and how to approach investments. This was brought home to me in a painful way when I did a pastoral internship at a church in my thirties. In one of our classes, one of the church elders gave a lesson on budgeting and finances. He talked about things like the importance of saving, having a plan for giving, and having an emergency fund. As he spoke, I was blown away—I had never heard these things before. I leaned over to one of the other interns, who didn't look nearly as impressed as I was feeling. "Have you already learned this stuff?" I asked him. "Yeah," he replied matter-of-factly: "My dad taught me about all this when I was a kid." "Must be nice," I thought to myself.

Moments like that one have come reasonably regularly as I've tried to catch up. So many of my adult years have felt like trial and error as I've stumbled through the dark, trying to make up for what I've lacked. Thankfully, the Lord is faithful to give us what we need, and he fills in all the gaps with his grace, mercy, and love. For me, one tangible expression of that has been the local church.

Immediately following the account of the rich young ruler in the Gospels, Peter casually reminds Jesus that the disciples have left everything to follow him. Jesus responds with a spectacular promise:

> "Truly, I say to you, there is no one who has left house
> or wife or brothers or parents or children, for the
> sake of the kingdom of God, who will not receive
> many times more in this time, and in the age to come
> eternal life." (Luke 18:29-30)

How can a person who has left their house, brothers, and parents in order to follow Christ receive "many times more" in this life? I believe that one answer to that question is the people of God, particularly in the local church. When we come to Christ, we are immediately adopted into a family with brand new brothers, sisters, mothers, and, yes, fathers. Though my earthly father wasn't and isn't around, in the household of faith I've inherited dozens of "fathers"—men who have instructed me, encouraged me, corrected me, prayed for me, and helped me in innumerable ways. It was through faithful, godly men in the church that I learned how to study God's word; how to lead my wife and children in family worship; how to disciple others; how to think about investing; how to give and receive godly encouragement and godly criticism; how to walk in humility; how to be a leader;

how to prioritize the church; and too many other things to name. This is a great kindness from God. And it encourages me to be that kind of man for others.

MARRIED WITH CHILDREN

Back when Blair and I first started talking, we were both struck by how similar our family backgrounds were. We were both adult converts who were raised in urban areas by single mothers. We both had fathers who were in and out of our lives. We both had a lot of brokenness and instability in our families. One of the things that excited us about coming together was the prospect of a fresh start. I'm a firm believer in the idea that just one godly married couple can have a lasting impact on many generations that follow them. As we looked in our family trees, we didn't see that couple. We believed that the Lord was giving us an opportunity to be that couple.

By God's grace, we recently celebrated ten years of marriage. In that time, the Lord has kindly given us three beautiful children. And I am so thankful that whatever story they tell when they get older, it won't be the same story that Blair and I tell about our fathers.

I'm repeatedly struck by how our kids see the world in ways that we couldn't have imagined when we were their age. Recently, I was talking to them about one of their older cousins. The conversation went like this:

Me: Your cousin Malik just had a son.
Our 5-year-old: Can we play with him?
Me: Maybe when he gets older. Right now, he's a newborn and can't really play.
Our 6-year-old: What's Malik's wife's name?
Me: Actually, Malik and his son's mother aren't married.
All the kids in unison: WHAT?!?!

Our 6-year-old: Not married?

Me: That's right.

(Long silence)

Our 8-year-old: How can they have a baby if they're not married?

(Brief pause)

Me: Who wants ice cream?

As I reflected on that conversation, I was struck by our kids' reality. In their precious little minds, it was simply inconceivable that two people who weren't married could have a child. For them, marriage and having children are inextricably linked, because that's all they know. It was so different—in fact, almost the complete opposite—to what Blair and I saw growing up! It was a moment that made me thank the Lord for his grace and marvel at how many lives he can transform in just one generation.

HOME IMPROVEMENT

With that said, I don't claim to have everything figured out by any means. As much as I've benefited from men in the church, I still feel like I'm playing catch-up in so many ways. As a father, it's a daily fight to resist my own sinful tendencies towards anger, apathy, and authoritarianism. One thing fatherhood has helped me to see more clearly than ever is the need for daily dependence on the Lord's grace. If I rest satisfied with yesterday's victories, I'll get steamrolled by today.

What I've come to realize is this: small steps of faithfulness pay off big over time. To use a baseball analogy, I can easily fall into the trap of swinging for home runs all the time as a dad, rather than being content with consistent singles, doubles, and triples. This error has sometimes showed up in our family worship. We've been doing family worship since our eldest was a newborn. Here's what it looks like: after dinner, I'll read whatever passage we're in that day. I'll expound on it, asking questions of the kids along the way. I'll always try to connect the passage to the gospel. We'll pray and then close out with a praise song or hymn. (By the way, any parent can do this. Including you. Ask an older father in your church for advice, grab a resource to help you if you need it, and just start.) For the most part, my children are engaged. But there are times when there are a million distractions, behavioral issues, or what seems to be disinterest. And for a long time, I was frustrated and discouraged whenever it felt to me like family worship wasn't a home run.

I spoke to an older pastor friend about this, and he told me the story of his son going off to college. After packing the last of his stuff together, father and son were just about ready to get into the car to head to the airport. As they started to leave the house, the son stopped in the living room and stared at the couch. The father asked what was going on, and with tears in his eyes, his son said, "Dad, for 18 years I sat on that couch each night as you led us in family devotions. Those times were very precious to me, and I'm going to miss them. Thank you, Dad." The father was moved, but at the same time was struck by the irony. This son, in terms of sitting still and focusing during the devotions, had been the most difficult child in the family. He would cause distractions and had to be disciplined often. On many occasions, the father had wondered if anything was getting through to him at all. And now, after 18 years, the father got to taste the sweetness of the fruit that had been cultivated through many years of faithfulness, even when it was hard. That long-term perspective is an encouragement to me as a dad, and not only in the area of family worship. In whatever I'm doing as a dad, I need to remember that it's not about my perceived home runs or even strikeouts—it's about God graciously bringing forth fruit over time as we serve him by faith.

Marriage and parenting are not easy for those of us who are sinners—which, of course, is all of us. But there are particular challenges for those of us who never got to see two married parents navigating the highs and lows of life together when we were growing up. So, to close, I want to speak to a particular group of men. I have you in mind if you grew up with an absent or abusive dad and you're a father now (or desire to be one). Like me, you're wondering how you're going to live out your calling as a father when your relationship with your own dad was so broken. I want to leave you with three things to consider.

God Has Given Fathers a Great Responsibility

The older our children get, the more clearly our flaws come into focus for them. In just a few short years, our kids will not be kids anymore, and we'll have to live with the ways that we will have shaped who they ultimately become, for better or for worse. If that sounds daunting, it is. In the letter to the Ephesians, Paul gives fathers some specific instructions:

> "Fathers, do not provoke your children to anger, but bring them up in the discipline and instruction of the Lord." (Ephesians 6:4)

As fathers, we've been given the primary responsibility to teach our children the ways of God. Our children don't belong to us. They are a special stewardship from the Lord, and we are called to train them in the way they should go. We are to equip and prepare them to face a world that for the most part despises God. If we have fulfilled our calling well, we should expect that our children will understand who

God is, what he requires of them and what he has done for them in the gospel. We should expect that our sons will know what it means to be a godly man and a godly husband and father, should the Lord provide those gifts. We should expect our daughters to know how to be godly women, and how to identify a man who will be a godly husband and father, should the Lord provide those gifts.

It's always important for us to remember that no matter how young our children are, God has designed them with souls that have incalculable worth. As the great Victorian preacher Charles Spurgeon put it:

> "The soul is an everlasting thing like God; God has gifted it with immortality; and hence it is precious. To lose it, then, how fearful! Consider how precious a soul must be, when both God and the devil are after it."[17]

As fathers, we have the privilege and responsibility to shepherd those precious souls. Who can read that and not say, with the apostle Paul, "Who is sufficient for these things?" (2 Corinthians 2:16). Paul said that as he considered the responsibilities of apostleship, but that sentiment certainly applies to fatherhood as well.

God Has Given Fathers All That We Need

Thankfully, Paul doesn't end there. Later on, as he continues his thought, he says:

> "Not that we are sufficient in ourselves to claim anything as coming from us, but our sufficiency is from God, who has made us sufficient to be ministers of a new covenant." (2 Corinthians 3:5)

---

17 *A Sermon (No. 92) Delivered on Sunday Evening, July 6th, 1856, by the Rev. C.H. Spurgeon At Exeter Hall, Strand.*

Just as God provided the necessary grace for the apostles to fulfill their role, so he provides the necessary grace for fathers to overcome neglect or abuse in our own lives in order that we may raise our children in the fear and knowledge of the Lord. It's like the old saying goes: "God doesn't call the equipped; he equips the called." God has not left us on our own to figure things out for ourselves. He's given us his word to teach us and correct us (2 Timothy 3:16). He's given us his Spirit to guide us and convict us (John 16:8, 13). He's given us our wives to help us and counsel us (Genesis 2:18; Proverbs 31:26). He's given us pastors to teach us and admonish us (2 Timothy 4:2; 1 Thessalonians 5:12). He's given us the church to pray for us and encourage us (James 5:16; 1 Thessalonians 5:11). In our pride, we may fail to use what's available to us, but we can't say that God hasn't given us what we need. We need to take full advantage of these graces from the Lord, so that our children might thrive and our fatherhood be a great blessing to them.

Our Fathering Is Not Our Righteousness

This last part is the most important. It's easy to hear the first two and say with gritted teeth and clenched fist, "Ok. I have my marching orders. I gotta get to it. Let's make it happen!" We believe the lie that this all depends upon us. There can be only two outcomes of this "Just Do It" approach: either we'll fail and be driven to despair or we'll succeed and become self-righteous, proud Pharisee-like dads. The way we avoid both of these is to remember that our righteousness is found in Christ alone, not in how well we think we're doing as fathers. We need to remember this line from the book *The Discipline of Grace* by Jerry Bridges:

"Your bad days are never so bad that you are outside of the reach of God's grace. Your good days are never so good that you are outside of the need of God's grace."[18]

Freedom comes when we recognize that God loves us with the same love with which he loves Jesus himself, whether we're doing great or failing miserably (John 17:23). We are not saved by being good men, good husbands, or good fathers. We're saved despite the fact that we'll never perfectly be the husbands and fathers we should be. When Jesus lived a perfect life, he fulfilled the law of God on behalf of each father who trusts him (Romans 5:19). And when he died on the cross, he paid the penalty for every sin committed by every man who believes in him (Colossians 2:14). And he rose from the grave in order that believers would draw strength from his resurrection power to enable us to walk in new ways that are not bound by anything, including our family history (Romans 6:4). This is our hope. And this is the power that enables us to walk in the calling that God has for us as men, whether we are single or married, whether we have kids or not.

We can always find hope as we remember the character of our heavenly Father. He knew exactly what he was doing when he sovereignly ordained our upbringing. He loves our wives and children more than we do. He loves us more than we realize. He is working out his purposes in our lives and in the lives of our families. If we ever find ourselves weighed down with the responsibility that God has given us, we need to preach to ourselves that we have a heavenly Father who loves us and who rules this world:

This is my Father's world:
O let me ne'er forget
That though the wrong seems oft so strong,
God is the Ruler yet.

---

18 *The Discipline of Grace* (NavPress, 1994), p 9.

This is my Father's world:
Why should my heart be sad?
The Lord is King: let the heavens ring!
God reigns; let earth be glad![19]

---

19 Maltbie D. Babcock, "This Is My Father's World" (1901).

CHAPTER 8

Jumping off the Merry-Go-Round

When my son was two, I bought him a ticket to ride the merry-go-round. He was enthralled by the look of the vibrant horses with their harnesses, the oscillating lions with carved manes, the circus elephants sporting a coat of arms, and the shimmering lights and bars painted to look like shiny brass. It all looked wonderful to his young eyes.

My son picked a cheetah to ride. I strapped him on and took my seat nearby on a reindeer. Now that I was up close, I noticed it was peeling, uncovering the white primer underneath. Once everyone was strapped in, the ride operator started the horizontal wheel. It was not what I recalled from my own childhood: rather than a smooth up-and-down glide, the ride was more forceful and bumpy.

I was snapped out of my internal processing by my son's wail.

He wailed so hard that I unstrapped myself and jumped up and, with my feet shoulder-width apart to keep my balance, I stood next to the cheetah, embracing my son to let him know everything would be ok. The ride didn't stop. And getting off was now impossible. We just kept circling.

That minute or so lasted several hours. When the merry-go-round eventually came to a stop, I unchained my son from the ride, his cheeks wet with tears. This felt nothing like the nostalgic memories I had from my childhood. We got as far from that ride as we could.

Life often works like a merry-go-round. Round and round the generations go, each much the same as the last one, everyone strapped in: some enjoying it, some hating it, many wishing they could get off but unable to. And many of us are strapped onto a beast called "fatherlessness." It carries us along a path that it has etched out over the course of many years. No one accidentally escapes their family history. We have to actively fight against fatherlessness continuing on and on from generation to generation. If left alone, life will be a series of coordinated circles that we have been strapped into by our parents and that we in turn will strap our kids into. We must get off the ride.

IN THE HOUSE

Biblically speaking, we should expect this fatherlessness merry-go-round. The consequences of sin most certainly can and will be felt by succeeding generations. Who I am today and who you are today will to some extent be the result of our upbringing, whether good or bad.

Many of us look back into our family history and what we see is a long line of broken marriages. There has been no stable, loving marriage in our family's past or present, and, as a result, our family has effectively normalized fornication. As a result of the breakdown of our families, and in view of the number of men who are unwilling to comprehensively father their children, we are left to wonder whether it is inevitable that the sins done by the parents must be carried on to, and in, the children.

Straight after giving the second of the Ten Commandments, which tells us not to make graven images or idols, God says:

> "You shall not bow down to them or serve them, for
> I the LORD your God am a jealous God, *visiting the*
> *iniquity of the fathers on the children to the third and*
> *the fourth generation of those who hate me."*
>
> (Exodus 20:5, my emphasis)

The consequences of the sin of the fathers were passed down through the generations because 1) they were making graven images and 2) they *hated* God. They were not worshiping or loving the true and living God but an idol—exchanging the glory of the immortal God for images (Romans 1:23). And so begins the generational merry-go-round. The younger generations feel the impact of the older ones' sins; and they will tend to repeat those sins, too.

So does this mean, then, that we are bound under a curse?

Often we neglect what comes after the passage about the sins of the fathers. Take a look at the verse that comes after the one we mentioned above and see the contrast:

> "You shall not bow down to them or serve them, for
> I the Lord your God am a jealous God, visiting the
> iniquity of the fathers on the children to the third
> and the fourth generation of those who hate me, *but*
> *showing steadfast love to thousands of those who love me*
> *and keep my commandments."*
>
> (Exodus 20:5-6, my emphasis)

This is the unresolved tension that runs right through the Old Testament: God will punish sin, and there is no escape from the generational curse of sin; *and* God will love the multitudes of those who love him. His very nature means he is committed both to visiting the iniquity of the fathers on the children and the children's children for those who hate him *and* forgiving iniquity and transgression and sin for those who love him (Exodus 34:7).

That tension is resolved only in the cross of Christ. Jesus became a curse for us (Galatians 3:13), breaking any generational sin that may have been passed down from those fathers who broke God's law (v 10). Jesus bore the curse that we might receive the blessing.

And he did this not only because we suffer some of the consequences of others' sins, but because we ourselves are sinners too. Jesus perfectly kept the laws that God commanded and that we could never keep; he went to the cross to be pierced for our transgressions; he was resurrected from the grave to prove that the Father had accepted his sacrifice as a worthy atonement for those who would trust in him. As we have come to believe in Jesus and be washed of our heavy burden of sin, knowing that Jesus has carried our griefs and sorrows (Isaiah 53:4), now we can rest in the fact that "if anyone is in Christ, he is a *new creation*. The old has passed away; behold, the new has come" (2 Corinthians 5:17, my emphasis). There is now no condemnation for those of us who are in Christ (Romans 8:1). Christ Jesus makes all the difference with and in us. His sacrifice is enough to destroy the curse which is found in us because of our sin. No sins that we've committed could overrule that perfect sacrifice provided by our heavenly Father. He loved us first, and now by his power we can love him in return. His love for us, shown through the gospel, keeps us from being cursed.

By God's steadfast love, we love God and are able to keep his commandments. We do this not in our own strength but because of the perfect work of Jesus Christ that has been accredited to us and through his powerful Holy Spirit who lives in us. And when we fail to obey God's commandments, we find, like the prodigal son in Jesus' parable, not condemnation but help in our time of need—help to turn our hearts back to God.

So no, we are not bound by a curse. Although we may have to grapple with the consequences of our father's sin, we do not bear any curse as a result of his sins. The cross broke the curse and now we get to start afresh, by God's grace.

That means we do not have to be defined by the consequences of fatherlessness. We are not bound to repeat those mistakes and pass on the consequences to another generation. The cross can break any consequences of the sin of the generation before, so that it is not felt by the generation to come. We do not have to worry about whether or not we are marked for failure just because our fathers failed in some way. Because of Christ, and the fact that he overcame the world, the stronghold is broken, full stop. Once he has saved you, you are no longer bound to march at the same rhythm that your parents or grandparents did. Now you can march in step with Christ as a child of God the Father. Once our Father becomes the dominant influence in our life, we will reflect him and his wisdom, and enjoy, by his Spirit, the power to walk in his ways.

You may have experienced great suffering because of your father's absence, but you are not cursed by nor doomed to repeat that pattern; and you can work through the residue of the consequences which have come upon you, and overcome them. In Christ, you have an endless bounty of goodness that you can glean from your perfect Father, and by God's grace you can pass that on to the next generation. That is how you get off the merry-go-round. The world tells us that there is nothing wrong with the ride, even if we notice the jolts, even as it makes us cry. The world gives us no resources to get off if we want to. But the gospel tells us that this is not how it should be, and gives us all we need to get off and stop the circle going round for another generation.

It is so easy to say, "If only I had had a parent who was godly, or stable, or responsible. If only my dad had been around. Then my life would look different." I have thought that. Maybe we take a moment to vent about that, but we cannot remain there. A pity party is an excuse so that we don't have to change. God chose our broken families for us—to change us, not to define us. Then God chose to give us a new family to transform us and put us on a trajectory towards true flourishing. We must not allow ourselves to sit in pity too long or spend our time blaming our parents. Yes, we acknowledge the truth about where our parent went wrong—and then we have to give it over to God. We have to wake up one day and say, "Yes, it is hard—yes, I have had a disadvantage—but I am not going to allow my parents' sins to become my own, and I am going to look to Christ, because he can undo those disadvantages in my life. I am going to ask my spiritual family, which he has blessed me with, to help me break free from my hurt so that I can begin to heal."

Cycles are hard to break. It is easier to ride and try to smile between the jolts, or just sit and cry, especially when we look around and see so many others clinging to their peeling giraffes and reindeer. What the gospel offers is a hope that does not come when we look within at ourselves or when we glance around to compare ourselves with others. I am not saying that we will never struggle with these things again, or that all will be fixed overnight. But over time, as we continue to strive and keep casting off our sin and putting on Christ's virtues, we will look back and find that there is much evidence of God's work of sanctification in our lives. By God's unending grace, we can remove ourselves from that cycle of sin and pain. We will notice that we look more like our heavenly Father than our fallen earthly father. "Beloved, we are God's children now" (1 John 3:2)!

THE MESS YOU LEAVE BEHIND

When Shai proposed to me on the steps of the Lincoln Memorial in Washington, D.C.—the same place where Dr. Martin Luther King Jr. gave his iconic "I Have a Dream" speech—while he was down on one knee, he talked to me about legacy. Legacy—leaving something different than what we inherited. When Shai and I married, we knew that we were taking a step away from, and against, the sinful pattern in our families. We were both the result of homes without fathers or marriages, but the Lord in his faithfulness had kept us pure through our courtship and engagement. I remember Shai telling me after we started dating, when I asked him what his thoughts were on physical boundaries, "You are my sister; I'm not going to treat you like my wife." He led well. We were walking in God's grace. We married, with the goal of seeking to model Christ and the church in our love for one another. We dreamed of what could be if God blessed us with children—how we could, Lord willing, raise our children in a home that would not be at all perfect but would be one that sought to be filled with love, grace, and good news. Are we still stumbling through some days? Yes—many days, in fact. And yet, the Lord has been gracious to us and our little family. Shai and I balance one another out and work together as a team in parenting. And there are some things Shai and I are doing now to bring about, Lord willing, a complete shift in our family line.

First and foremost, we are both here. Recently, Shai had a talk with our two boys about how, when they turn 18, they need to be prepared to move out of the house. As a mom, I would never have thought to say that to my babies. I would be tempted to say, "Stay forever." And yet I recognize how important those conversations are because we are raising men. How many men have never had that conversation because they never had their dad? How many men don't know what it means to grow up because they have, from the best of intentions and the most loving of hearts, been coddled by their moms? So many instances like this have taught me in real time the importance of there being a mother and a father in the home.

Shai prioritizes leading our family in worship, taking the children through the Scriptures and catechisms, and singing and praying together. When I'm with the children, I try to be winsome as we work through conflict, trying to get to the heart to show my children their need for the good news, without overdoing it. Many times we've had to apologize to our children because we've sinned against them—this, too, is intentional, showing them that repentance and forgiveness are a daily reality for God's children. We pray that, through these conversations, our children will be pointed to the Lord. We recognize that now they are nine, seven, and six, we don't have a lot of time left with them—they will be in our home for ten more years, give or take. We pray that in the end, they will see that our desire is to be a blessing to them, helping them be formed into upstanding, godly people who are able to thrive in ways that we have struggled to and taken time to, because they have grown up in a different relational setting than we did.

If you are a parent, I pray that you can have juicy conversations with your child or children about the fatherhood of God, the beauty of marriage, the necessity of the gospel, living a God-honoring life, and compassionately caring for others. I pray you will have them when you are driving to school, sitting at the dinner table, or strolling the hypnotic aisles of Target with a kid in a red cart.

One thing we all know is that talking is not enough. Even more important than what we say, knowing that our children are watching us, is what we do. So, we seek to be careful about what we model in front of our children. We do this not to be phony but to walk in the Spirit's self-control. We strive to not argue in front of our children or discipline them out of anger, although at times we have failed. And it bears repeating that when we do sin against them, we ask for their forgiveness. I pray that my children will see in me not a perfect parent but a dependent one. I am praying they can know that, when they need help, they can call out to God for mercy—and they can always come to us.

All the time, I have to fight against the temptation to give my kids everything I didn't have when I was growing up. I didn't have housing stability growing up, and I desire it for my children—but I can't worship stability. If I think that in order for them to flourish the children need to be participating in several extra-curricular activities, I am showing them that this is essential to their identity, and I am teaching them to worship an idol. Truth is, having a stable mother and father in the home does more in a child than a particular house or hobby. I have to constantly cast over my own idols and be reminded of those essential things that God is calling me to as a parent. My job is to point them to the one who says to tell the children to "come." If I try to step in and fix all of their problems—if I try to be a supermom—I'm eclipsing the opportunities they have to get to know their heavenly Father personally. Parents make terrible gods and so do their idols. If we want to raise self-controlled, godly children, we must be self-controlled, godly parents. Like Hannah did in giving over her longed-for son Samuel to serve God once he was weaned, I have to get out of the way and entrust my children to the Lord.

ALL OF US
I realize that you may be reading this with a wistful heart and a sinking feeling, because you are a single parent. You may desire to have a partner to help build up the beautiful children you have, but that is not what has panned out. Remember,

the grace that overcame your sin is sufficient to go to work in your circumstances, whatever they are. There is no family set-up that does not still require God to be at work, making up for our flaws and failings; there is no family set-up that is too messy for God to be at work in. Yes, he created us to raise children in a home with a mom and a dad; but the ideal is not to become an idol—either for those of us who are blessed in that way or those who (very possibly through no fault of their own) are not. None of us are sufficient for the task of parenting; he is, always.

There are so many godly single parents, and they often don't receive much recognition. But God sees you single mothers herding several children into the car on Sunday mornings despite all of the challenges that come with bearing the load alone—and doing so because of your love for God and the church, and your desire to model that to your children. God sees you single fathers sitting with open Bibles after a long day of work because you want to teach your children about the Lord and how important the Scriptures are, even when you are exhausted. When I think of the faithful parents in my church, there are many single moms who come to mind—they are some of the most mature women in our church, who are bearing a heavy load of caring for their children's overall well-being. I see them fighting to be Christ-like, trusting the Lord with unmet expectations, catechizing and lovingly shepherding their children, and doing this all as they engage with their child's father who doesn't know Christ yet. And God sees that, too.

Life's hard. Parenting is hard. If this is you, trust the Lord to give you the grace to press on each day and make the best use of the short time you have with your children. Keep going. You are building a legacy.

And if your kids are grown and out of your home, or if, up to this point, children have not been God's plan for you, you can still build this legacy of a generation that knows what godly family looks like. Adoption has secured a family for us in the body of Christ. This means that we are all called to be spiritual mothers and fathers to those who are younger in the faith than us. There are many opportunities to walk with those around us, whether they have their parents in the home or not.

A sweet example of this is a dear sister who I used to attend church with, named Trish. Trish is not waiting for marriage to create a legacy. She has fostered a couple of young ladies who are in their late teens and who had been waiting for many years to be fostered or adopted. She has taken them into her home and cared for them. Even as they have come of age and moved out on their own, she has still been active in their lives, serving as their forever family so that they always have a place to call home. She has come along as a place of comfort, stability, and influence in these young ladies' lives as she points them to the Lord. She has been the way God's grace has broken into these relationally broken lives.

Another example is of our good friends Brian and Heidi Dye, who have served inner-city Chicago for about 20 years. Over the course of those years, they have had around 200 young men live with them. During their stay, they have discipled these men, many of whom do not have their fathers present in their lives. The Lord has not given them biological children yet. In the meantime he has given them a great legacy through the many young men who have come through their doors and met Jesus. God has allowed them to have a great legacy of serving young men in their community. Some have been converted and have gone on to build healthy marriages, have their own children, and even pastor churches. That's a legacy!

When older men lock arms with younger men and older women with younger women with intentionality, it can have a ripple effect that lasts for many generations. What legacy do you want to leave as a testament to the work of God in your life?

THE EMPHASIS OF OUR MENTORSHIP

Whether you are married or single, or parenting biological, fostered or adopted children, or mentoring at your local church, here, fairly briefly, are four values Shai and I strive to live out as we engage in our Father's work in training the children entrusted to our care.

1. Devotion to God's Word

We know that heaven and earth will pass away, but God's word will not (Matthew 24:35). Our Bible is our handbook of sacred words inspired by God to help lead us to dig deeper in our knowledge of God.

John Piper, in his book *A Hunger for God*, says:

> "The greatest enemy of hunger for God is not poison but apple pie. It is not the banquet of the wicked that dulls our appetite for heaven, but endless nibbling at the table of the world."[20]

The world is preaching to us all the time, in rapid ways. God speaks to us through his word. We must be devoted to listening to him more than we listen to the other voices that crowd in on us.

We must familiarize ourselves with the Scriptures so that we can live out what they say. We must study them rightly. We must know this word so that we can overcome error and grow in truth. That way, the word will be on our lips when we give counsel and mentor our children. Speaking God's word to

---

20 *A Hunger for God* (Crossway, 1997), p 18.

them is more powerful than any other words we can come up with. The word of God is the truth which helps us understand God's thoughts and ways. More than wanting our children to know our own ideas and ways, we want them to understand God's ways so that they might know him.

The more that we are meditating and studying God's word, the more it will pour out of us when we are around others. We will be leaving nuggets of truth with them which, we pray, will outlive us—truth that they can continue to pass along to those they pour into.

2. Dependence in Our Prayers

Constant communion with God is a treasure we received the moment we came to Christ. We have the privilege of approaching God's throne with all of our requests because God's ears are attentive to the cry of his people.

The more we walk with Christ, the more dependent upon him we should become. As time goes on, we become more aware of our need for Christ as we become more aware of the frailty and sin in our heart. This causes us to cry out in dependence to God regularly.

We often think the person who is most mature is that way because they are strong. The truth is, the most mature among us are those who recognize how weak they are and come to God with a child-like faith. So, when we see those sinful patterns in us that were in our parents, it is not enough to say, "I don't want to repeat what I see in them." We must recognize the error, confess it to God, and ask God to help us repent so that we can begin to practice new, healthy, holy patterns. The more regularly we depend upon Christ, the more we are communing and clinging to him. Dependence leads us to worship.

Not only should we model prayer, but we should also pray for our children. I pray for my kids almost every day—

praying for that which only God can do. I know that only the Lord can save and change them. I am praying that the Lord would bless them by giving them godly families who carry on a legacy of godliness. All of these things that I desire for my children are things that the Lord must do. I know that if I do not pray for them, then I am either being complacent or somehow believing the lie that I am more influential than the great I AM. God is a great Father who gives perfect gifts that we cannot (Matthew 7:11).

3. Doxology Through Hymns

I recently started teaching my children the lyrics to "Great Is Thy Faithfulness." Truthfully, I'm learning some of the lyrics with them. I want my children to have an arsenal of truth in song to cling to both now and when they are far from me, so that as they grow older or even when I'm long gone, they will know how to worship God in song. These hymns, which have been passed on to me, need to be passed on to them: "What a Friend We Have in Jesus." "Blessed Assurance." "At the Cross." "Jesus Paid It All." "It Is Well with my Soul."

These hymns and others cultivate hearts that bask in God's glorious truth, lifting our souls into a deep affection for God. When God's word dwells in us richly, one of the things we do is sing (Colossians 3:16). Make your home one filled with singing so that as your children get older, worship will permeate their hearts, hold them steady in the harder moments, and one day flood their own households too.

At times, some of the hymns my Momma used to sing, which she learned from her father, come to mind. She would sing spirituals like "Standin' in the Need of Prayer," or "Amazing Grace," or "I Am Determined to Walk with Jesus." Other times, she would just sing, "Yeesssss... yessssss...

ye-esssssss… yessssssss… yesssssssss… yeeessssss, Lord." It was a way to say, "Not my will, Lord, but your will be done."

I am committed to singing these songs to my children so that they continue to be passed on to future generations.

4. Deeply Loving Toward People

What is our Bible reading, praying, and singing if we have no love in our hearts for others? We are like a clanging cymbal (1 Corinthians 13:1-3). God has called us to love image-bearers. Scripture says if we do not, then we don't truly love God (1 John 4:20).

The second greatest commandment is to love your neighbor as yourself (Mark 12:31). When we have little love for God, we will have little love for the people he created in his image. When we have a vibrant love for God, we will be compassionate and merciful towards others. The Good Samaritan shows us that it costs to love our neighbor (Luke 10:25-37). Love is more than words or an emotion. Love is the act of showing mercy to those who come across your path and may be different than you.

We are called to do good to everyone, especially our brothers and sisters in Christ (Galatians 6:10). This is why, as we saw in chapter 4, those who have not had biological fathers in their lives should be comforted and nourished by the church. God has given the body of Christ this responsibility. If you haven't had your father in your life and you have had to scratch and crawl your way to understand how to live a healthy, functioning, Christ-glorifying life, maybe it's time to pour that hard-won knowledge into someone else. In parenting and mentoring, we pull others in to observe what we are doing, not because we have it all figured out but because God may use us to build up an area that is lacking in another. Our legacy should be one of love, displaying the outpouring of our lives for one another that we see exemplified in our elder Brother Jesus.

GROWN-ISH

Although the four values I have listed above are not exhaustive when it comes to mentorship, they do assist in our spiritual growth and the growth of those we are mentoring. All that we do should be done for the glory of God and be the result of our love for Jesus, with the aim that our expression of love may show Christ to those we are serving. As you walk in the fruit of Christ's labors, by faith cycles will be broken, and that will ultimately have an impact on your children, your church, and your community. You do not need to stay on the merry-go-round of generations of fatherlessness. Even as you wrestle with its consequences, either in your own life or in the lives of those around you, you can break the chain. The generation above us may have been relationally broken; ours need not be, nor does the one after us need to be. The cross has broken the curse and freed us for maturity. We are growing up in Christ. The Spirit dwells in us to move us up and move us on—to build a legacy that has an eternal impact and that outlives us.

CHAPTER 9

Coming Home

They say that "home is where the heart is." Home is that place where we do not feel like a stranger. It's where we are authentically known and unconditionally loved. It's where we belong. It is our crucial point of reference for knowing who we are. It gives us a sense of security, rest, and belonging.

Where is home for me? Home has always been a hard place to define. It's never been where my father was. When our family would pack our best clothes into a suitcase to travel home for Christmas or Thanksgiving, we were never going where my dad resided. And still today, I realize that I don't feel at home yet with my biological father, although we do talk and are slowly getting to know one another. But it is hard work. The phone conversations are brief, and they are awkward at times as we try to figure out what to say and what to ask. We are strangers trying to get to know each other after years of not knowing that each other existed. I'm not rushing it. I don't have high expectations. I am just happy to know the truth. We will see where it leads.

My other dad, Dee, and I talk on average once every week, even though as I was growing up, he didn't feel like home. I am grateful for him now—grateful because I know that he knew the truth all this time and chose to love me anyway. From when I was aged 18 onwards, he has sought to be a more intentional part of my life. Although he is an imperfect picture, his choosing me does remind me of my perfect Father. I still wrestle at times with the question of which would have been better—to have known my biological father from a young age but possibly not had much of a relationship with him, or to have had Dee, who's not my biological dad but now treats me as though he is. And there is always the question of how deep I should go to try to make up for lost time. Maybe I should just keep things light and be thankful for what I have, even though I have always desired more.

Sometimes I vacillate between desiring a home here and settling into the reality of my heavenly one. I am learning to rest in the fact that God has chosen not to give me a human father who will meet all of my needs. He has a purpose in all this, even if I do not yet fully understand why. One thing I do know for sure is that my present trials are preparing me for an "eternal weight of glory" which will outweigh all of these difficulties (2 Corinthians 4:17). This is my reminder, when I am tempted to waver and be consumed by "Why?" questions, that I *am* on a journey home—just not to a location that can be quantified by four stucco walls, three bedrooms, or a street name that includes the words Avenue or Road. The greatest desire in my heart could never be satisfied by an earthly father at all.

HAPPY DAYS

Although the Lord is with us now and has adopted us now, in one sense he is somewhat still removed. I do not mean that he is not with us—he is revealed in Immanuel. I do not mean that we do not really have him—we do. We have his Spirit, dwelling in us (Romans 8:9). What I do mean is that right now, we can only see him dimly:

"For now we see in a mirror dimly, but then face to
face. Now I know in part; then I shall know fully,
even as I have been fully known."

(1 Corinthians 13:12)

When we are with him, we shall know him comprehensively.
We will be able to behold him, face to face. He will remove
the hindrance of our sin, and we will have not one inch of
distance, no cloud, nothing between us and him in the new
heavens and new earth. He will be a fully present parent, and
we will be able to grasp it. The faith, hope, and love we have
now will all melt into love for our everlasting Father. Can
you imagine? God will honor his promise to us. Our elder
Brother, Jesus, will usher us into the presence of our Father,
and there will be no more hindrances keeping us from our
true home—the place we really belong.

We are on our way home, and we are not there yet. But one
day we will be, as our Brother told us:

"In my Father's house are many rooms. If it were not
so, would I have told you that I go to prepare a place
for you? And if I go and prepare a place for you, I will
come again and will take you to myself, that where I
am you may be also." (John 14:2-3)

There is a family dynamic in heaven which consists of God
the Father, Jesus our elder Brother, and redeemed humanity—
us—as siblings all being fueled by the Holy Spirit. We will
legit live happily ever after with our family, "born, not of
blood nor of the will of the flesh nor of the will of man, but
of God" (John 1:13). And this is no fairy-tale.

So sit with me as we finish, and look with me toward our
home—the place where we'll be with our Father.

SOUL TRAIN

In our new home, God our Father will provide all that we need. In this life we have many cares and concerns—but in the new heavens and new earth we will have no more concerns nor anxious cares. We will know complete peace and joy in God's presence as our souls are satisfied in him. There will be no more pain from fatherlessness. There will be no more mourning or tears. God will do permanently what every natural father should seek to do and yet no natural father can ever completely do: he will wipe every tear from our eyes (Revelation 21:4). He will protect and provide for us. If you are in Christ, Scripture is speaking of your future when it promises:

> "He will dwell with them, and they will be his people, and God himself will be with them as their God. He will wipe away every tear from their eyes, and death shall be no more, neither shall there be mourning, nor crying, nor pain anymore, for the former things have passed away." (Revelation 21:3-4)

There will be no more tears shed over fathers who were missing from our basketball games, dance recitals, weddings, or—fill in the blank! This pain will be a distant memory, eclipsed by the joyful affections of living in our Father's glory.

All that we need will be fulfilled in God. There will be no need for a temple to worship in because God will be the temple. There will be no need for the sun or moon, since God's glory will be the light in heaven. There will be no more destruction, or danger, nor anything detestable (v 22-27). There will be no more turmoil and chaos, symbolized by the sea, in heaven (v 1): and "the one who conquers will have this heritage, and I will be his God and he will be my son" (v 7).

Best of all, as we persevere to the end by faith, we conquer, and as a result we have a heritage—and our heritage is not a place but a person! Our heritage is to have God as Father.

He will be our God, and we will be his sons and daughters. When our Father is our greatest joy, then even when all else is taken away from us, we still fully and eternally have what we most value. Home is where our Father is, and we're journeying toward it.

GLEE

The psalmist says:

> "You make known to me the path of life;
> in your presence there is fullness of joy;
> at your right hand are pleasures forevermore."
>
> (Psalm 16:11)

Only in God's presence is there fullness of joy. This means that our joy now is scarce in comparison to what it will be when God replaces all our sin with perfect holiness. Now we still have to fight past our fluctuating emotions, our very real grief, and our sin. When we are with God, all of those barriers will be taken away. The temptations we have from the devil, the world, and our flesh will be obsolete. We won't have other emotions competing for our joy. We will have only the influence of the Holy Spirit and the joy of being in the presence of our Father and his Son.

There may never have been any joy in your earthly home, but there will be fullness of joy in our heavenly home simply because God is there. He will provide himself for us, and once he has taken away all of those "no mores," there will be no interference to our delight.

FAMILY AFFAIR

Our Father's home is our family home. Of course, our adoption into his family doesn't begin in heaven—we have already thought about how we are a family now. The difference is that our family will be perfect when we get home. There will be no more twitter battles, family hurt, disagreements over secondary issues, denominational segregation, or temptations to ignore Christian charity. Our sorrow will turn to joy. When we are all in heaven, we will be able to worship together and enjoy the fullness of Christ as one glorified body.

In John 17:20-23 Jesus expands on the unity he spoke of earlier in chapter 14 when he prays:

> "I do not ask for these only, but also for those who will believe in me through their word, that they may all be one, just as you, Father, are in me, and I in you, that they also may be in us, so that the world may believe that you have sent me. The glory that you have given me I have given to them, that they may be one even as we are one, I in them and you in me, that they may become perfectly one, so that the world may know that you sent me and loved them even as you loved me."

This oneness refers to a profound unity that will exist perfectly among believers when we are with God. We strive for it now, but our sin gets in the way. No Christian is an island. Through our unity and love to one another, we testify to the world that the Father sent the Son and loves us as he loves the Son. We are to seek to show on earth what will be in heaven. Our unity now should be like the unity shared between the Trinity. The oneness between the Trinity is eternal. They are of common mind and mission, with an unqualified mutual love. This oneness does not mean sameness. The Father is not the Son; the Son is not the Spirit—they are three distinct Persons yet one in essence. They share a perfect unity and yet there is diversity among them. Similarly, there is diversity among us (Revelation 7:9), yet we are all united together under one Father forever. Our roles will change, but our family will not.

In heaven there will only be one Father. Our heavenly Father is drawing our attention upward to his always present, never changing, faithfully comforting role in our life. His heavenly fatherhood never dies out. Since God is never given to fallibility, his glory only seems to grow as we look on. Once we are home, all the scales will fall away from our eyes and we will behold the full beauty of our Father.

FATHER KNOWS BEST

I wonder if part of the reason some of us have been ordained to be without our fathers now is to enable us to depend upon our always-Father a bit sooner. When we have a lack, it provides an opportunity for us to seek God and depend upon him to provide for us. The more in need we are, the more dependent we realize we must be. We can be like the women who anointed Jesus' feet, who loved him dearly because she had been forgiven much. The difference between her and the religious leaders whom Jesus was eating with was not the extent of her sin, since they were all sinners just the same, but her recognition of her need (Luke 7:44-47). The truth is that those who do not have their fathers and those who do both have the same deepest need—to be a child of God. But maybe in the lack of not having our fathers, we can see that need a bit more clearly, and we can cry out to our heavenly Father a bit more fervently. And we can look forward to being home with him a bit more keenly.

ARE WE THERE YET?

For now, though, we are on the journey. Our challenge is to trust him until that day as we navigate this fallen world. But of course he has not left us alone to do that.

When Jesus was in Gethsemane the night before he died, knowing that his time had finally come to die, he prayed. He was greatly distressed and troubled. His soul was sorrowful, even to the point of death. He was so overwhelmed with sorrow that he fell on the ground and belted out a prayer to his Father. He said, "If it be possible, let this cup pass from me" (Matthew 26:39).

He knew that he would have to be betrayed at the hands of sinners. The perfect, spotless Son knew he would endure so much sorrow and suffering and pain. Never has there been sorrow like this. He knew that he would experience temporary separation from his Father as he took on our sin. He was going to bear the full force of the wrath of God out of love for us who are now children of God.

It was in the midst of this unthinkable pain that he cried out in his native tongue of Aramaic, "Abba" (Mark 14:36)! *Abba* is a term that a small child would use to refer to their father. "Daddy" is the closest that English comes to it. Some push back on saying this because they see "Daddy" as irreverent; but with all due respect, that *is* basically what the word means. It is a term of endearment, showing an intimate trust in God's fatherly care. Jesus cried out to his Father when faced with bearing his cross, and so we can and ought to cry out to our loving Father when faced with bearing ours—saying, like Christ, "Abba, Father, your will be done."

> "For you did not receive the spirit of slavery to fall back into fear, but you have received the Spirit of adoption as sons, by whom we cry, 'Abba! Father!' The Spirit himself bears witness with our spirit that we are children of God, and if children, then heirs—heirs of God and fellow heirs with Christ, provided we suffer with him in order that we may also be glorified with him." (Romans 8:15-17)

The Spirit of Christ allows us to call out to God, "Abba! Father!" *Abba* is literally the cry of the child. Because we have been adopted, the Spirit bears witness with our spirit that we are children of God. The Holy Spirit not only makes us God's children but makes us aware of that. The Holy Spirit places within our human spirit a comforting conviction or an inward confirmation that we belong to him. Not only do we belong, but we have been made heirs of God and fellow heirs of Christ. This means that Christians will inherit all that God has promised Christ—his home will be our home. Can you imagine?

In order to access the glory, we must suffer with him. The particular trial of not having the presence of a biological dad around brings about its own suffering, which sets us up to fix our eyes more intently upon the glory that is to come. Having God as Father doesn't take away all of the pain of not having our biological dad, but it does help us wrestle through that pain and come out on the other side more dependent upon our unchanging Father. I appreciate that God doesn't sugarcoat or pretend as though there will be no challenges in this life. Jesus said that there would be hard things, and yet he comforts us and prepares us for heaven, our forever home.

Sin ruins beautiful things, but grace restores what's been broken, making it better. Those who cry, "Abba, Father" know that God will not leave us in our distress, because he didn't leave Jesus in his. We know that although Jesus suffered and died, he was resurrected by the power of God. The Father kept his faithful promise to him of resurrection. He will keep his promises to us.

So what does this mean for us saints who journey through this fallen world? It means that fatherlessness doesn't have the final say. It doesn't define us, and it doesn't defeat us. The longing we have for our father is but a shadow, testifying to the fact that we were made for another Father. The longing for home that we have, which has not and cannot be fulfilled here, shows that we were created with another home in mind. Of course, we would love to have a present, loving earthly father in our life—but what we have with God is better. We are going to the King's house, and he is our Father.

Find that Father and you have all you need, forever. Find that Father and you have a forever family. Find that Father, beloved—the Father who really found you first—and you know you are headed for home. Home is where my Father is, and so with that certainty among the oscillating complexities of life, and with that joy amid the distressing pains of life, and with that hope amid these heavy momentary afflictions, I journey on. Because I am my Father's child.

Acknowledgments

Thank you to my husband Shai, who I get the pleasure of running this race alongside. I am grateful for the way you lovingly support me as I use the gifts the Lord has given me. What a blessing that by God's grace and through faith we get to walk out what we did not see growing up. Thank you for writing a chapter sharing your story and encouraging the men. Thank you for how you have been there through all of the difficult news I've had to sift through over these past couple of years. Your nudges of encouragement to choose love and forgiveness has helped my growth. I understand my Father's love because of how quick you are to lavish love on me. I love you, and may God bless our marriage and the legacy that we seek to leave.

Thank you to our children, Sage, Maya, and Ezra. You are all so special to me. As you know, we are not perfect parents—we've only been at this for nine years, so we have a lot to learn. Thank you for being so patient and forgiving. Thank you for the tight snuggles, encouraging notes, and family sleepovers. I pray that no matter what comes in this life you will never forget or question the love your mommy and daddy have for you. I also pray that, as you see God more and more, you would one day make the choice to have him as your heavenly Father.

I am so grateful for Momma, a believing grandmother who, as she would say, "prayed me out of Hollywood, and into the arms of Jesus." I am indeed her legacy. Hallelujah, she is with the Lord!

Thank you Mother, for making significant sacrifices. I have tried to think back and put myself in your shoes for just a bit, and I know it was much more difficult than I could capture in thoughts or words. I do not know what it is like to experience such loss, with your father passing away when you were nine and your son passing as an infant. I pray that God the Father would encourage you and cover you with his saving peace. I pray for you often.

Thank you to my dad Dee. I am so grateful for you. Thank you for never pulling back on your love. Thank you for your words of encouragement. Although as a child I did not always appreciate them, today I am so grateful for your encouraging words. Thank you for doing what you could and for intentionally showing up and being present from when I was 18 and onwards. I love you and Momma V. Dad, I pray for you both often.

Thank you to my biological dad Jewel. What a wild ride this past year has been. We met in person for the first time right before the country shut down for the pandemic. There is still so much for us to learn about each other. I am so grateful that I know the truth and that you are in my life now. Not only have I gained a father but also aunts, uncles and cousins. Thank you all for welcoming me with open arms. Dad, I pray for you often.

To my sister Brande, I love you and am grateful for you. We have been through so much together and yet the trials and trauma do not define us. God determines who we are. Because of Christ we are overcomers. I am so grateful that the Lord has saved you and given you a desire for his word just a few years ago. Your love for the Lord and his word is an answer to my prayers and also Momma's prayers. You are Momma's legacy. May you be convinced more and more how much you are loved by our Father.

Thank you to all of the churches I have been a member of and all of the faithful Christians I have had the privilege to observe and be discipled by. God never gave me just one person; rather he encouraged me through a community of believers. There are too many to name here, but all you who have had a hand in shaping me, I thank you.

Thank you to my editor Carl Laferton, as well as the entire staff at The Good Book Company. Carl, they say less is more but I read somewhere that it's better to have more words than less when writing. You were definitely on the receiving end of the "more." Ha. Thank you for helping me make the book what it is today. Your notes and suggestions have made this book better.

I wrote this book to encourage the fatherless. So I want to acknowledge the many saints out there who are persevering despite not having their dads in their life. To you who are fighting through the hurt and pain to make much of our God and Father, this book is for you. May our Lord Jesus Christ encourage you and bring much fruit through your labors. May he surround you with a caring church. May you excel in Christ, may you be convinced of your spiritual adoption which has made you a son or daughter of God, and may you one day find a fatherless child who you can pour into.

Finally, may we all as the church participate in that "true religion" James speaks of, which includes caring for the fatherless (James 1:27). I pray this book pushes us toward that holy work.